# THE RELIGION OF
# A MATURE MIND

# THE RELIGION OF
# A MATURE MIND

BY

GEORGE ALBERT COE, Ph. D.

JOHN EVANS PROFESSOR OF MORAL AND INTELLECTUAL
PHILOSOPHY IN NORTHWESTERN UNIVERSITY.

AUTHOR OF "THE SPIRITUAL LIFE: STUDIES IN THE
SCIENCE OF RELIGION."

CHICAGO   NEW YORK   TORONTO
FLEMING H. REVELL COMPANY
LONDON AND EDINBURGH
MCMII

# DEDICATION

# PREFACE

The discussions that compose this volume have to do with perhaps the least considered phase of the profound change that is taking place in the religion of the western world. The theoretical aspect of this transition has been carefully studied. As far as doctrine is concerned, we know somewhat precisely whence we have come and whither we have thus far gone. But the corresponding transformation that is taking place in personal and practical religion, and in the modes of its propagation, has received much less attention than it deserves.

A considerable part of the Christian world appears to be either drifting with this uncharted current, or else protesting against drifting; those who seek to understand and to utilize the new set of conditions are as yet in the minority. There is, indeed, a somewhat general disposition to assume that religion, as distinguished from doctrine, lives in a changeless world by itself, apart from the tides and currents of thought. In the sense that theology is a product more than it is a source of life, this assumption is not entirely without justification. Yet just because doctrine is a product of life, it is also to some extent an index of life. We may safely presume that any era of doctrinal agitation is likewise an era of agitation, normal or abnormal, in other vital functions.

This presumption will become established fact for any one who will take the trouble to compare contemporary and recent church life with that of our grandfathers. It is not merely ideas that germinate, blossom, bear fruit, and decay, but also modes of feeling, of expression, of propagandism, and of daily conduct.

This aspect of religious progress is the hardest one to accommodate ourselves to. The inertia of habit and of institution is even greater than that of thought-systems. Men are always demanding to be assured that new ideas do not touch questions of conduct or of Christian experience, and theological conservatism supports itself to a considerable extent by leaning upon the conservatism of personal and practical religion.

Theory and practice have, in fact, a common root and a common sap. This truth is well illustrated in the relation of modern biblical scholarship to the Christian conception of life. We have been many times assured that the new learning does not take away anything that was ever essential to Christian living. This is doubtless true, but the use made of it is misleading. For our notion of what is essential to Christian discipleship does change from time to time, and with it our aspirations and our conduct. Just now it is being modified in the closest relation to the growth of knowledge concerning the Scriptures. When an undeveloped historic sense, for instance, permitted men to place upon the same plane of spiritual authority the words of patriarch, Levitical lawgiver, psalmist, prophet, and the Christ, modes of life were accepted as Christian that could not now find toleration. The new conception of a developing revelation has so focused spiritual authority in Jesus that men no longer find it easy to wrest Scripture to the service of their arbitrary desires and practices. Thus, the higher biblical learning and a higher standard of life have come to us hand in hand, each one, doubtless, promoting the other.

The task that I have set myself in these discussions is that of formulating, not the complete life of a Christian, but only the central dictates of practical wisdom in a set of emergencies that we must face in connection with the characteristic thought-movements of our time. These movements I shall not undertake to defend. For, however much remains to be done with respect to their logical grounds, boundaries, and affinities, their essential justice may be said to be already established. I refer particularly to the following group of ideas and tendencies: the demand that the scientific method be employed in the study of religious as well as other facts; the application of the theory of evolution to the whole of man's nature; belief in the immanence of God in nature and in man; the employment of literary and historical methods in the study of the Scripture; the social interpretation of the teachings of Jesus; the increasing emphasis upon love as the supreme quality of the divine character; finally, the recognition of likeness to Jesus, irrespective of dogmatic affinities, as the adequate and only test of Christian discipleship. If these conceptions be true, we must prepare ourselves not only for revising

much of our theology, but also for reconstruct-
ing almost the whole scheme of Christian
living.

This reconstruction has already gone far
enough to make possible a few generalizations
concerning its tendencies. Three great
changes, it seems to me, are coming over the
practical life of Jesus' disciples. First, the
Christian life is being simplified; second, its
ideals are being socialized; third, its motives
are being intensified. The substitution of a
simple for a complex creed appears at first
sight to imply sacrifice of truth, but in the
end we discover that what we have lost in the
range of our pretensions we have gained in
the stability of our faith. Similarly, the
abandonment of a scheme of rules in favor of
a simple principle or motive appears like let-
ting go something of virtue, but we find that
it is progress from letter to spirit, from that
which kills to that which makes alive. Simplification of the issues of life, moreover,
makes it harder for us to dodge them, or to
thin out our consecration.

The socialization of our ideals, likewise,
seems at first sight like turning our backs on
salvation and heaven. But in reality it merely

reproduces the life of Him who thought that even being in the form of God was not something to be grasped after, but made Himself of no reputation, and took upon Him the form of a servant. Finally, the simplification and the socialization of life both tend to intensify its motives. When life becomes simple, attention focuses upon essential goodness; when it is socialized, the whole weight of human sympathy is brought to bear upon the conscience of the individual.

The total result is bound to be a new type of aggressive Christianity. There is neither clear thinking nor practical wisdom in the habit, which some have fallen into, of representing Christianity as threatened with spiritual paralysis through the thought-tendencies of our age. A more real danger is that of making Christianity appear to be always on the defensive. When the rapid movements of modern life make us nervous; when faith is regarded as resistance rather than as aggressive assimilation; when fresh conceptions are treated with suspicion until they compel a reluctant assent; when, in short, the church moves by impact from without rather than from its own vital impulses; then, indeed, comes the real danger of spiritual paralysis. The world must learn that the Christ is no mere expedient, but rather a creative principle; that he does not merely judge the world, but is rather the source and embodiment of its life; that Christianity is not a mere governor upon the engine of human progress, but even the motive power of the whole movement.

The title of this volume was chosen, first of all, in view of the fact that several of the discussions contained in it originated in practical talks to college students concerning various difficulties that arise in passing out of the religion of childhood and of youth into that of maturity. A further reason for the title is my conviction that the supreme practical task now facing the Christian world at large is parallel to that of the college student. The church at large has to emerge from the dogmatic and emotional attitudes essentially characteristic of youth into the equilibrium of a spiritual maturity which shall include at once intellectual freedom and illumination, emotional health and practical aggressiveness. The somewhat hortatory tone of some of the chapters is due to the practical use originally made of the material. I have chosen not to

remove this feature, not only because practical
interests are still the main concern, but also
because the wisdom or the unwisdom of what
is said will be revealed not less by the immediate application than by the logical reasons
adduced in its favor.

GEORGE ALBERT COE.

Evanston, Illinois, September, 1902.

# CONTENTS

13

# MODERN MANHOOD

In precisely the same way, religion, in its
ideal conception, is always and everywhere the
same.    The rude ceremonies and symbolism
of the lowest tribe are inspired by the same
fundamental needs as our more spiritualized
worship.    Yet the higher is only germinally,
or ideally, present in the lower.    The actual
religion of any age or of any people cannot
possibly be transferred unmodified to other
peoples or other ages.

> "Each age must worship its own thought of God,
>     More or less earthy, clarifying still
>     With subsidence continuous of the dregs;
>     Nor saint nor sage could fix immutably
>     The fluent image of the unstable Best,
>     Still changing in their very hands that wrought."

There is, accordingly, a sense in which we
may say that religion needs to adjust itself to
the men of every new generation.    This is
only another way of saying that each generation must be religious for itself; that religion,
being a vital process, is incapable of being
handed down, like houses and lands, from
father to son.    Abraham could not possibly
have communed with God in just the way that
the Apostle John did, as, on the other hand,
John would hardly have called a man religious

In precisely the same way, religion, in its ideal conception, is always and everywhere the same. The rude ceremonies and symbolism of the lowest tribe are inspired by the same fundamental needs as our more spiritualized worship. Yet the higher is only germinally, or ideally, present in the lower. The actual religion of any age or of any people cannot possibly be transferred unmodified to other peoples or other ages.

> "Each age must worship its own thought of God,
>   More or less earthy, clarifying still
>   With subsidence continuous of the dregs;
>   Nor saint nor sage could fix immutably
>   The fluent image of the unstable Best,
>   Still changing in their very hands that wrought."

There is, accordingly, a sense in which we may say that religion needs to adjust itself to the men of every new generation. This is only another way of saying that each generation must be religious for itself; that religion, being a vital process, is incapable of being handed down, like houses and lands, from father to son. Abraham could not possibly have communed with God in just the way that the Apostle John did, as, on the other hand, John would hardly have called a man religious

# CHAPTER I

## MODERN MANHOOD

The qualities that go to the making of a man are, in a sense, eternal and changeless. Manhood always means something different from childhood, and something distinctly opposed to unmanliness. Even a savage, who measures virile courage by bloody deeds, has in him a prophecy of nobler loyalties and enthusiasms.

Yet only in the ideal conception can manly qualities be said to abide unchanged from stage to stage of progress. The courage that enables an Indian warrior to disregard his own pain makes him also ruthless toward others. The strength that we admire in him is that of an extreme egoism which, found in us, could not possibly be called manly. Humanity, as realized in concrete men, changes from age to age. Though it contain at all times some glimmering impulse toward the full stature of a man, this last is always an ideal; it is never a completed possession.

# MODERN MANHOOD

who followed merely the ideas and practices of Abraham.

Religion does not come down from heaven as a finished thing to which men must adjust themselves: rather, it arises through their own inner impulses and longings; these are instruments whereby the Father prevents men from being contented until they come into communion with Him. Proceeding thus from within outward, religion requires readjustment as continuous as the struggle for life itself. A developing humanity implies a developing religion. Faith must ever make new discoveries of its own essential wealth, and of its inherent adaptability to the whole of developing human nature.

We have fallen upon a time when this readjustment cannot be left to unreasoned impulse. The age is self-conscious and critical, possibly too much so; in any case, there is no prospect that the people will ever surrender the right they now claim to conscious and deliberate choice in matters of religion. We need, therefore, to ask, What are the characteristics of modern manhood, and what new or special demands do they place upon religion?

The manhood of to-day has received a

peculiar stamp from three great historical influences.   The first of these is

*The Growth of Science and the Diffusion of
    Knowledge.*

We might almost say the birth of science
and the beginning of popular knowledge.   For
the changes that have arisen from the adoption of critical, inductive and experimental
methods make of modern science something
practically new in kind as well as in degree.
Not less remarkable is the transformation in
the mind of the ordinary man.   For him to
dare to ask questions is something new in the
world, and for him to command the answers
is still newer.   In the making of man, few
modern forces have been as influential as the
printing-press and popular education.

The growth of scientific knowledge, and
particularly improvements in the methods of
research, have changed the whole feeling of
men toward nature and toward many things
connected with the problems of human destiny.   Men have ceased to be afraid.   There
is no longer any such thing as a natural por-
tent.   Comets and earthquakes, storm and
pestilence, warts and moles and monstrous

growths—these awaken no apprehension of the operation of supernatural powers. In the very yesterday of history, men felt insecure of themselves because magic and witchcraft were still believed in. It was still commonly believed that nature is pervaded by capricious and incalculable factors. We have our own unsolved problems, as our fathers did, but they awaken little mystic presentiment, and no fear. We do not catch our breath at the thought of what may be, but boldly take to pieces every new phenomenon, certain in advance that it harbors no hobgoblins and no secret of how to transmute base metal into gold or old age into youth.

Religion cannot appeal as successfully as of old to the sense of mystery. Man has lifted the veil of creation and gazed at nature face to face. That gaze has made him feel his own importance. He has dared to know, has not been blasted for his curiosity, and henceforth nature is for him simply so much pliant laboratory material. He has learned

"To laugh at Jove's old-fashioned thunderbolts,
Could he not also forge them if he would?"

This spirit is not limited to men of science. It has taken possession of the common

people, and they are flouting mysticism, and
assuming an air of intellectual aggressiveness
amounting almost to arrogance.   Intellectual
oligarchies and monopolies are thoroughly
broken down.   The common man assumes
both the right and the capacity to know anything that interests him.   He feels no hesitation about questioning accepted beliefs.   He
proposes to act from self-chosen notions of
the meaning of life.   In view of the influence
of tradition and authority in other times, one
may well be astounded at the extent to which
untrained men assume to think about the profound problems of human destiny.   The buy-
ers and sellers, and even the toilers, have
assumed a right to think for themselves.   As
a result, they have largely ceased to find anything terrifying in doubt and skepticism, or
anything attractive in conformity.   But such
men merely intend to apply, according to their
capacity, the same spirit of intellectual aggression that distinguishes modern science from
its forerunners.

We may summarize the effect of modern
science and of the diffusion of knowledge by
saying that, through all grades of society,
fears and mystical presentiments have been

allayed; intellect has become self-confident and extraordinarily active; men boldly accept the responsibility of doubt and dissent; and authority, whether in doctrine or in practice, has largely yielded before individual opinion.

A second important factor in the making of modern manhood is found in

*Modern Invention and the Resulting Extraordinary Extension of Man's Control over Nature.*

Knowledge has been turned into power, and nature has become a sphere for the exploitation of human enterprise. The effect produced upon the spirit of man by the ability that modern science has bestowed upon him to predict heretofore incalculable natural events, is heightened by his newly acquired control over powers to which in other days he could only submit. The old type of awe and resignation is gone forever.

The spirit of modern invention differs in one important respect from that of ancient invention. Men have always been inventors, and some of the early inventions have had as important consequences as any of the later ones. He who first invented a wheel, or a harness, or a sail, or a water-wheel, put into the hands of his fellows an instrument of incalculable benefit. But none of these early triumphs of inventive genius inspired men with such a sense of superiority to nature, and with such an ambition to control her forces, as is commonplace with us. Nature as a whole was still a vast unknown against which it was madness for puny man to match his power. To harness an ox or even a waterfall is merely to utilize one of nature's finished products. The modern inventor goes beyond all such makeshifts by appropriating nature's own laboratory and pressing her elementary laws into his service. To generate steam and electricity for our own use is to exercise an almost demiurgic authority. Such wonders set men dreaming. Shall we not sometime travel through the air; drive our machines by direct application of earth's magnetic currents; control the rain clouds; manufacture our food by chemical processes directly from inorganic elements; communicate with the inhabitants of other planets?

Men who do and dream such things experience a redistribution of the elements of character. The direction of the redistribution has been variously described. Sometimes the spirit of the times is called materialistic because its attention is so fixed upon things. But everything depends upon what men see in the things upon which they fasten their eyes, and certainly the modern man beholds in nature something more than brute things of sense, and he aspires to something greater than merely having things, or merely using them for the purchase of passing pleasures. If we measure the higher life of a generation by the amount of attention it gives to education and learning, to literature and the arts, to the amelioration and prevention of human suffering, to the improvement of men's relations to one another, to the development of social and civil institutions, and to religion— then materialism is not a characteristic mark of our age. It seems, too, as if the very greatness of our tools and of our ambitions tends to raise the mind above mean conceptions of life. Who has not met mechanics who appear to have been ennobled by familiar contact with powerful yet delicately adjusted machines? Who does not know that the enthralment of business men in their business is due largely to a fascination which makes of commerce a mighty game in which the pleasure of winning outweighs the stakes? A part of the race, even in this western world, is still engaged in the struggle for mere existence. But this is less and less the case as modern life unfolds. There is nothing irrational in the prediction that present tendencies will bring to the dawn a day in which the whole of work will be transformed into something more like play than a contest for food.

Sometimes the age is called utilitarian, and certainly the modern man does see in things chiefly instruments for promoting human ends. Yonder flow the lazy tides of ocean; some day they shall become toilers in the workshop of humanity. The radiant energy of the sun shall run to and fro upon our errands. The very changes of the seasons shall fill our reservoirs of energy. Yes, our typical man is the practical man, and the important question with him is, ''What is it good for?'' If this is utilitarianism, then the age is utilitarian. But the utilitarianism that means the same as devotion to material ends as final is not characteristic of our age.

This brilliantly successful appropriation of nature has added to our sense of the value of this life. We no longer feel that we are pilgrims and strangers passing through a disagreeable country because it contains the only road to a better; we feel more and more at home where we are. We are not in an enemy's country; on the contrary, the world belongs to us, and we propose to cultivate it, and apply the produce of it to human ends. We are outgrowing the habit of longing for another world, while more and more arises a wish that we might live here for a hundred or a thousand years. The world-weariness of an occasional pessimist, decadent or blasé idler, is a mere incidental product; the modern world as a whole, at least the western world, feels young. The prevailing sentiment is that the present is good; that the future is to be better; that progress is the order of the world; and that to have a share in the universal movement is worth while.

Thus our new control over nature gives us self-confidence, inspires a practical attitude toward all things, makes us this-worldly rather than other-worldly, and gives zest and buoyancy to the work of the world.

The third important formative influence upon modern manhood is

*The Growth of Popular Government and of
the Social Consciousness.*

Closely corresponding to the new attitudes
toward nature are those of the democratic
spirit toward dignities and prerogatives. Not
only has a freer play of individuality resulted
from the removal by the modern state of the
ancient pressure from above, but the individual
has also acquired a habit of making ever
larger and larger demands upon life. The
unit grows ever bigger. Upon himself, upon
his neighbor, and upon his God, man lays increasing obligation. The church's loss of
influence with certain classes of the population
is probably due in part to the increasing extent and stringency of the demands placed
upon her.

From of old, religion as well as the state
has come to men as a compelling power from
above. Its characteristic words have been,
"therefore," and "thou must." The creed
has been reached by syllogism, and syllogisms
are not formulated by popular vote. The
commands and advice of religion, likewise,
have been those of a master addressed to a
servant. But the democratic spirit leads the

individual to look within himself for his "must" and his "ought." Syllogism ceases to frighten him as soon as he becomes bold enough to question the premises; and as for the commands, he will do what to his own sense seems good, and then he will deliberately "take the consequences."

If religion is to make an effective appeal to such men it must approach them in a new way; not the way of compulsion or of show of authority, but of friendly interest, inspiration, and helpfulness. This fearless, self-assertive man must learn that, in order to be his whole self, he must be religious; that God is not and never was a foreigner to any member of the human race, but is present in all men as the inspiring source of all that is worth while. In place of pressure from above must come impulsion from within; for the supposedly external master must be substituted the unquestionable authority of the God within the soul itself.

The difficulties that democracy has brought to religion are partly offset by the birth of a new social sense. Democracy and pure individualism cannot possibly be reconciled with each other. For, in the nature of the case, my claim to be a source of authority and an end of social institutions stands upon precisely the same level as the similar claims of my fellows.    Thus it has come to pass that the world of to-day, whatever else it may doubt or deny, acknowledges one kind of law that does not need to be voted on; namely, the obligation of brotherhood.

Some friends of religion have queried whether this remarkable growth of the sense of obligation to men does not tend to obscure the sense of obligation to God—whether the modern world is not in danger of substituting morals for religion.    A just perspective into the mind of the modern man, it seems to me, would reveal an exactly opposite tendency. The wave of democracy has, indeed, thrown the individual back upon himself.    But, striving to be himself, he discovers that no man lives to himself; that the center of gravity of his own life lies outside him as a mere individual.    The next step will be to try whether the social sense can realize its ends without likewise transferring its center from men considered as finite, temporary phenomena, into some eternal, divine world.    Surely, to start the movement from pure individualism toward this goal involves no small gain to religion. This, at least, is certain: the brotherhood idea commands us by an authority that is not questioned. If it can attain its ends without religion, why should it not do so? In any case, let us push it toward its own good goal, certain that an effort to fulfil the second of the great commandments will not weaken the authority of the first. Possibly, in the age that is dawning, God will make of the newly invigorated social sense a chief instrument of his own self-revelation.

Such being the influences that tend to give a special stamp to our age, it remains to ask

*How these Things Affect the Modern Man's Religion.*

Here, as before, it is possible to speak only of massive tendencies. Many an individual lives largely apart from them; many more are affected by them without knowing it. The official utterances of a whole communion may condemn them at the very moment when the mass of its membership is under their sway. The statements that follow, accordingly, should not be tested by reference to picked individuals or communities, or by comparison with official formulas, but by the actual habits of conduct, speech, and institutional life that may be observed, particularly in the centers of modern life.

Such observation will show, in the first place, that fear has practically ceased to be an influential factor in religion. Preachers are no longer accustomed to appeal to it as a motive, probably because such appeal is found to be useless. The modern man cannot be scared by the thought of death or of the judgment, and if he could be, the modern code would require him to conceal his terror. We may attribute this to callousness of heart, or to doctrinal looseness, or to the three influences just described. I believe that, apart from the increasing emphasis upon love as the supreme quality of the divine character, the chief cause of the decay of religious fear is found in these three factors. This result, too, is inevitable; the human material upon which religion works has permanently shifted; men's knowledge and power and social and civil status preclude the effective use of these older persuasives. To lament the effect is to distrust the cause. The better way is to trust to the uttermost the forces that make for a higher civilization. Possibly men's new confidence in themselves, in the world, and in life, has in it a germ of faith; possibly the casting out of fear will turn out to be one road to the perfect love of God.

In matters of belief and of conduct authority tends to disappear, and in its place comes an appeal to the heart, the conscience, and the reason. The Vatican Council's decree of papal infallibility appears at first sight to contradict this statement. But the fact of life is revealed less surely by a doctrine decreed by a majority vote against strong opposition than by actual practice. During these thirty years no incident like that of Canossa has tested the real authority of the popes. The two incumbents of the Roman See have been tolerant advisers, and even within this short period of thirty years we have beheld a not inconsiderable tendency to assimilate modern facts and views rather than combat them. The increasing liberty within the ranks of the clergy is a further indication of the same tendency. It is not improbable that the world has heard the last *ex cathedra* utterance upon questions that could possibly bring papal authority to a real test. While the temper of the faithful is that of sincere reverence, this temper itself probably depends upon the absence of the sense of compulsion.

As to the Bible, its influence to-day rests chiefly upon the self-evidencing wisdom and goodness of its teachings. Formerly men reasoned as follows: Miracles and prophecy prove the Bible to be a divinely inspired revelation; being inspired, every word of it is true; this or that statement is contained in the Bible, is therefore true, and to disbelieve or to disobey it is to flout God. To-day this syllogistic procedure fails to convince. Men ask, "How do I know that these premises about miracles, prophecy, and inspiration are true?" Few men have the equipment for searching out these things, and of those who have it, not a few reject the ancient syllogism. What, then, shall the common man do? The day is past when he can stake his religion upon the "say so" of his neighbors. The modern spirit impels him to come at things for himself. What he actually does is to test the contents of the Scriptures by such standards as seem to him inherently just. There is much in the Bible that he does not understand, or does not find any use for, and this he dares to pass by; but there is also much that he can use, irrespective of the syllogism of authority, and this he proposes to take advantage of, whatever its source.

This attitude denotes a departure from the formulas that grew out of the Reformation, it is true; but, after all, is it not just the plain man's way of applying in his own life the Reformation principle that the individual soul can come directly to God? This self-reliance ought to be tempered by the historic sense, of course. Democracy itself rebukes arbitrariness in the citizen as well as in the ruler. Yet, after all, if the Logos, the Word in whom was life, lightens every man coming into the world, why should we shrink from assuming that the ultimate authority in religion is some sense of the right and the good whereby the Eternal communicates himself to us? In any case, the modern man with whom we have to deal shows no tendency to return to the former view.

The growth of scientific method has made men extraordinarily cautious about making assertions that cannot be substantiated by exhibiting appropriate facts. That responsibility begets conservatism is well recognized in practical affairs, and it is true of the intellect also. A man who feels the responsibility for his beliefs will naturally be chary of assent, if not, also, of dissent. The conservatism of intellect imposed by scientific method has been largely misunderstood. Because men have been less ready with answers to questions about divine things, the age has been called skeptical and radical, whereas it is more conservative than radical, and too conscientious to be flippantly skeptical. There is a frothy and obtrusive surface of life where radicalism does assume to be the fashion, but the mass of society is too serious for that. Men feel something of the burden of having to settle things for themselves. This is one reason why they find it possible to get along with so much less in the way of creed than their fathers deemed indispensable.

Creeds are being pruned, also, in order that they may bring forth more fruit. A practical age calls for a practical religion. The questioning attitude does not affect the ancient duty to do justly, love mercy, and walk humbly. From disputation and doubt the heart turns gladly to ask what we ourselves can do to make the world worthy to be

the work of God.   The emphasis has shifted
to conduct, and particularly to the relations of
a man to his fellows.   In this respect the
spirit of the age and the spirit of the Master
have much in common.   The lines are being
drawn more closely than ever before between
selfishness and self-seeking.   Not merely how
we spend, but also how we get; not merely
how much we give, but also how much we
retain; not merely how little harm we do, but
also how much good we might do; not merely
how much is mine, but rather how the "mine"
can best serve humanity—these questions are
coming home alike to capitalist and to laborer,
to him whose wealth is in things, and to him
whose wealth is in capacities of muscle or of
mind.

This demand for a practical religion, and
particularly for one of active service of fellowmen brings discredit upon the self-centered
seeking of emotional satisfactions.   Of what
use is emotion unless it leads to action?
And if action is the end, why not go directly
toward it?   This is the spirit, formulated or
undefined, of a large element both within and
without the churches.   It is reinforced by a
very natural reaction against the emotional

excesses of other days, and by a better understanding of religious phenomena whose mys-
teriousness used to be accepted as evidence
of the special interposition of the divine hand.
It is true that a considerable proportion of the
membership of churches that are accustomed
to cultivate religious experiences still adheres
to the earlier view.   God is looked for in the
rushing mighty wind of feeling, or in the still,
small voice of some personally appropriated
satisfaction.   But, in spite of the many voices
that call upon us to look back at the mighty
works of God in other days, the emotional
form of religion is less esteemed and less cultivated from year to year.

If this lessened regard for religious emotion means that something less than the whole
man is to be exercised by religion, then are
we moving toward an extreme no less unten-
able than the emotionalism of other days.   It
is impossible to have values without feelings.
The age does well when it protests against the
one-sidedness of emotional religion, and particularly when it insists that religious ends are
always social, never merely individual.   But
we shall some day realize that a fully social-

ized religion must be one, not merely of dry acts, not merely of illuminated thought, but also one warmed and colored by abundant feeling playing back and forth between man and man, and between man and God. A socialized religion is one of communion of soul.

All the emphasis placed by our age upon the dignity of man, and all its attempts to socialize our life, make it easier to believe that an ideal manhood would be the supreme information as to the divine character. And so the manhood of to-day, though with only a half-consciousness of what is happening, is being led by its own most approved motives back toward Him who not only proclaimed but also lived the principle of human brotherhood. In a new way the Son of Man is asserting his mastery over men.

It is one of the paradoxes of history that the process of outgrowing authority should lend impressiveness to the very thing in the interest of which authority was invoked. For ages men fancied that the supremacy of Christ must be enforced by compulsion, whether that of fagot and stake on the one hand, or that of irresistible syllogism on the other. It seemed incredible that the great logical and institutional buttresses could be removed without causing the building to fall. But the modern world is demonstrating that Christianity is a building not made with hands. It is a life that supports itself by its irresistible power of assimilation. We have but to come into contact with Jesus to discover that we cannot escape him. He has an extraordinary power of asserting himself within us, and not merely without. It is as if he had somehow succeeded in commingling his being with what is deepest and best in our very selfhood.

Hence it is that the religion of our age is calling, "Back to Christ!" Back from theoretical Christs to the concrete, historic figure which embodies for us our best thought of ourself and our best faith in God. The Man of Nazareth comes to us, as to the men of his own age, in no royal or priestly splendor. He has no such external beauty that we should desire him, no external compulsion with which to overwhelm us. He relies upon nothing beyond the intrinsic creativeness of his own personality. This revelation of him in his true simplicity has brought him to the heart of

the world as arguments, institutions, and ceremonies could never do.

If we ask whether the religious tendencies
of the modern world are, all in all, wholesome,
no better answer can be given than this: The
heart of our age clings to the Christ!

# THE SCIENTIFIC SPIRIT IN
## MATTERS OF RELIGION

# CHAPTER II

## THE SCIENTIFIC SPIRIT IN MATTERS OF RELIGION

Happily for both science and religion, attempts to "reconcile" the two have ceased to be fashionable. Both sides to the old controversy have found a more excellent way, and both resent the imputation that there is any hostility to be removed. This is due largely to a clearer understanding of the difference between science and religion, as to both purpose and method. Science investigates phenomena and their relations; religion fixes its faith to the invisible reality that is the ultimate ground of all things visible, the changeless heart of all this flowing universe. Again, science deals solely with matters of fact, while religion deals with values. The one is satisfied if it can discover the actual order of events; the other seeks to transform human life in accordance with an ideal. Science has to do with the mechanism of the world; religion, accepting the scientific description of the machine, goes on to ask what it all means, and the religious impulse rests not short of the conviction that, as our own machines are devised to minister to our human life, so the machinery of the universe exists for a benevolent purpose.

As far as it goes, the question of its finality being waived, this division of labor marks real progress.    There is, however, a problem with which we still have to wrestle.    It is the

*Problem of Adjustment Between the Scientific and the Religious Function.*

It has to do, not with reconciling one belief with another, but with combining one impulse with another.    The religious and the scientific function must be exercised by the same individuals; and furthermore, both undertake to deal with what is true.    If religion should be reduced, as some would have it, to mere æsthetic or ethical emotion; if its recognized sphere should be the imaginary rather than the true—some other side of our nature taking sole account of the real universe—religion would soon evaporate.    The breath of its life is its consciousness of penetrating through mere appearances to something that can be absolutely relied upon because it is the reality of things. If we are to have religion at all, then, we must recognize religious truth. Thus, religious truth-seeking and scientific truth-seeking are required to stand side by side, and if religion is to be more than a specialty of experts, the two must be so related that they can live together in harmony in the same individual.

The newer problem is to discover a natural adjustment between the spirit or mental attitude of science and that of religion. This takes the place of the former debates over supposed conflicts between geology and Genesis, or between evolution and the Bible. The later task is more fundamental and more difficult than the earlier, since it concerns, not the logical relations of ideas, but the co-ordination of the various elements of personality.

Is the scientific mode of approaching truth opposed to the religious attitude of mind? If so, men who lean toward science will lack reverence and spirituality, while men who lean toward religion will want scientific rigor. In each individual one impulse will tend to suppress the other, and society will be divided into warring factions.

The result would be scarcely less deplorable if the two should be merely indifferent to each other. For now the individual would suffer the same schism as society suffers if the two are opposed to each other. "When I go into my oratory," said some one, "I forget my laboratory; and when I go into my laboratory, I forget my oratory." That is, what religion, in the moments devoted to it, declares to be the reality of life becomes unreal during the hours of the daily occupation. Conversely, as a condition of worshiping God, one must renounce for the time being all the tests by which one ordinarily assures one's self of the actual as distinguished from the imaginary. It is not in human nature for a normal man to live such a double life. What touches the man in one sphere must not be dishonored in the other.

Men who fancy themselves in this predicament generally seek escape by yielding up one side of the nature a sacrifice to the other. In nearly every case it is the religious side that is sacrificed, and for a very obvious reason. The methods of the sciences are more definitely organized than the corresponding modes of religious thought. Religion cannot measure and weigh the objects of its thought, or experimentally reproduce its facts for purposes of investigation. Again, religious thought has clung longer and more tenaciously to authority and to dialectical and speculative schemes. Whenever evidence has failed, its tendency to assert that faith can take the place of evidence in producing a reasonable conviction has also given it the appearance of double dealing. Finally, religious thought has, not unnaturally, assumed the attitude of an attorney rather than that of an investigator. While the man of science is required to find out something that he does not know, the religious thinker knows his conclusion in advance, and merely seeks means of proving and defending it. The very preciousness of religion has rendered difficult the absolute candor that gives to all facts and considerations the exact weight that belongs to them, irrespective of their bearing upon a conclusion that we desire to establish. When the dearest things of the heart plead on any side of a question, one would have to be almost superhuman or subhuman not to render a prejudiced decision. There are, of course, scientific as well as religious prejudices, yet they have no such eloquence as that of the religious instinct.

The realization of these things has produced a certain non-commitment in matters of religion among persons of scientific occupations and sympathies. Sometimes it calls itself agnosticism, a term that ought to be limited to a certain philosophical theory of knowledge. To extend it to a mere mental attitude that results from experiencing a disagreeable situation tends to confusion of different things. The non-committal attitude is not a part of philosophy. Nor is it a permanently tenable resting-place for the mind. The religious instinct and the intellectual instinct are both fundamental to our nature. The demand to know what the universe is, and the demand to find firm standing-ground for our whole personality, must somehow discover that they are not opposed to each other, or even indifferent, but co-operative, if not actually akin. Possibly the religious spirit can be as much at home in the laboratory as in the house of prayer. Possibly the scientific spirit is needed in religion as much as anywhere. I believe that it can be shown that the pure flame of scientific zeal burns the oil of a truly religious reverence and aspiration after God, and that, conversely, not only can religion accommodate herself to the scientific spirit, but she even requires this spirit for her own health.

*The Religious Element in the Scientific Spirit.*

When Lord Bacon enumerated the *idola*, or illusion-producing prejudices from which we must free ourselves if knowledge is to become fruitful, it probably never occurred to him that, with slight modifications, his words might be used as a religious exhortation. Yet it is true that science and religion alike demand that we shake off the bonds of personal inclination, of social convention, of habitual modes of speech and thought, and even of hereditary impulse, in order that we may come directly and unwarped at truth and reality. The most characteristic thing about modern science, in fact, is not its wondrous insight into the constitution of the universe, but rather its spirit of self-abnegation and of devotion to ideal good. The scientific spirit is greater than all its products. Patience, exactness, the repression of haste, the silencing of desire, the postponement of conclusions that seem near, not seldom the sacrifice of the dearest children of

one's thought, and not seldom, too, the daring
to contradict an incredulous and intolerant
world; in short, the counting of self as nought
that one might by all means win the truth has
been the price of scientific purity and progress.

It has been remarked that purity of heart
is as necessary in science as in religion, and
it is certainly true that only those who become
as little children can enter into the fulness of
this kingdom.   Here the lazy man, the con-
ceited man, the self-willed man, and the insin-
cere man are out of place.   As scientific men
we must love nothing merely because it is
ours; the only ground for attachment to any
idea is that it fits things as they are.

There are, of course, proud and self-willed
men of science, just as there are inconsistent
Christians, but it remains true that the spirit
of science is essentially opposed to self-will
and self-indulgence.   It requires a surrender
to something higher than self; the desire to
know becomes something more excellent than
any form of self-seeking, even the joy of a
certain losing of life in which, nevertheless,
behold we live.   At its highest this becomes
indistinguishable from the glow of religious

devotion.    It is as if the truth were saying to men, "If any man would come after me, let him deny himself," and "Whosoever loses his life for my sake shall find it." Whoever heeds this call becomes an apostle, one separated and sent out on a holy mission.

The consecration of the modern intellect to ideal aims should be recognized as a religious phenomenon.    A really scientific age cannot be also a materialistic age, for science does not worship things, but ideals.    Its passion is for truth, and truth is a temple of which the senses are only the vestibule.    There is not only an analogy, but also partial identity between the scientific spirit and the religious. The passion for truth is nothing less than a dim and partially developed act of worship toward the God of truth.

Down in its deepest heart, accordingly, we may assume that the scientific spirit is an inspiration from on high.    It is a visitation from Spirit to spirit.    In order to say this, we need not conceal the decided deviation of modern science from the state of mind traditionally held up as that of a spiritual man. Neither religious teachers nor men of science have adequately realized the meaning of loving

God with all the mental powers.   And so it has come to pass that men have put asunder what God has joined together in the texture of our faculties.   Devotion to the ideals of science has been assumed to have no inner relation to devotion to other ideals.   As a consequence, any deviation of scientific knowledge from the dogmas of religion has had an undue tendency toward alienating the investigator from the religion of his fathers.   The conservative element actually present in all devotion to the ends of knowledge, being unrecognized by either party, was robbed of its just effect.

This is one of the underlying causes of the paralyzing effect so often experienced by young men upon their first contact with science.   The actual presence of a religiously conservative factor in intellect itself, however, has had something to do with the equally marked tendency of men, at first alienated, to return after a while toward the simple religion of their childhood.   They effect this return, let it be noted, not by any relaxation of scientific methods or ideas, and not in any large degree through the logical compulsion of any part of scientific knowledge, but rather through a maturing recognition of the spiritual element present in their aspirations from the start. Professor Shaler, for example, says that it was a more profound grasp of science itself that brought him back from an early excursion into religious negations.    (The Interpretation of Nature, Boston and New York, 1893, IV.).    Similarly, Romanes, who made the entire circuit from belief to unbelief and back again to Christian faith, never abandoned his early ideals, but only corrected them by a more rigorous analysis of scientific procedure, and enlarged them by his growing experience of life.    It was, so to speak, the discovery of the man in the investigator that effected the change from a negative to a positive attitude. (Thoughts on Religion, Chicago, 1897.)

If religion comprehends all the ideal aspirations of the human soul, then not only are the scientific and the religious spirit not hostile or indifferent to each other, but, on the contrary, the two breathe the same breath of life. To the doubting man of science we can say: "Your devotion to truth is already a part of the spiritual life.    You are paying homage to something in the invisible world which you have made your ideal.    To us this ideal is

more than a creation of our own minds; it is
the ultimate reality and the Father of our
spirits, whose mind is the final home of truth.
O come, let us worship and bow down!''

## The Scientific Element in the Religious Spirit.

The man who invented the saying that
ignorance is the mother of devotion was not a
psychologist; for it requires only ordinary
insight into the human mind to perceive that,
though ignorance may create and perpetuate
particular beliefs and forms, it does not
create the religious impulse itself.    The
instinct for religion cannot be separated
from the impulse to know.  This is not
to say that religion is primarily or chiefly
an intellectual function.  Religion is not due
to a desire to explain the world, except as the
need of explanation enters as a factor into a
more comprehensive need.  But the aims of
intellect and those of religion do certainly
have a common focal point.  Intellect aims to
know things as they are; religion seeks to
adjust the whole man to ultimate reality.
Both turn the attention from mere appearance,
and from the merely changing things of sense,
in order to find rest of mind in something un-

changing and eternal.  Within the confused manifold of experience each seeks in its own way to find a principle of unity and of order. Through all the uncouth pictures painted by the religious imagination, and even through all the devout gnashing of teeth against philosophy and science, the religious heart has been seeking to square itself with reality. Religious men may sometimes be half-hearted in their loyalty to truth, for religion as well as science can partially misunderstand itself, but all the interests of religion are against self-deception, and in proportion as the religious spirit grows mature, it candidly, courageously, and constantly turns its face toward truth and whatever leads thereto.

The presence of this intellectual factor in the religious instinct brings it to pass that religious faith finds one of its tests in its attitude toward what claims to be newly discovered truth.  A living faith desires to increase knowledge; a faith that is contented with what it already has is moribund.  Again and again during the last century was Christian faith brought to this test.  Upon the announcement of a new discovery in geology, biology, or biblical research that was supposed to con-

tradict accepted doctrines, two parties at once
formed within the circle of the churches.
One party promptly denounced the new views,
proclaiming with a loud voice that to accept
them is to surrender the faith.   The other
party went quietly at work to see whether, in
reality, a new discovery had been made; if so,
how it was to be interpreted; and finally, how
the existing doctrine must be modified in view
of the new knowledge.   These were the true
champions of faith.   Through them Christianity demonstrated its vitality by a rapidity of
assimilation never before witnessed.

Religion, then, requires the same candor
and aspiration for truth that inspires science.
It not merely tolerates the spirit of science,
but rather includes it.   Nor is this all.   The
specific method of modern science, or the
principles of it, have a direct application and
use in religion.   We are coming to see that
religion, as well as pure knowledge, needs the
empirical spirit.   For religion includes thinking, and thinking is most fruitful when it sticks
close to the facts of experience.   Now, religion itself is first of all experience.   Whatever
of mystery or of transcendent reality it contains or conveys, it is a set of determinable

impulses and aspirations, feelings and desires, tendencies to do and to believe, and apparent responses to the same on the part of a supposed divinity.   These are the reality of religion—a reality that is raised above all the uncertainties of speculation.   Fixing our attention upon it we can say, "One thing I know," and the effect will be wholesome for both theology and everyday living.

The employment of empirical methods in the study of religion undoubtedly departs from the beaten pathway of theology.   The ambition of theologians has been to prove by strict demonstration how the things of the soul must be, while science humbly inquires how they are actually observed to be.   In order to see the necessity of the latter method, we do not need to condemn the former.   It has its historical justification, and should not be lightly judged by circumstances very different from those of its origin.   Then, too, even when we contrast the certainty of experience with the uncertainty of speculation, we should bear in mind Aristotle's distinction between the things that are most certain in themselves, and those that are most certain for us.   The value of facts lies in what they reveal, and it is entirely conceivable that the same truth should be revealed in more than one way. Leaving open, then, the question of the possible success of the traditional method of theology, let us ask whether something different is not called for by the circumstances of our time.    There can be but one answer to this question.   Rightly or wrongly, the men of this generation do not feel sure of the older method.   If I mistake not, the unrest of the time is less a revolt against the content of traditional beliefs than anxiety to find some way of being sure of something.   The great question is not whether this or that doctrine is true, but rather where a starting-point is to be found, and how we are to distinguish the true from the false.   In other matters men begin with the observed fact.   The student of nature moves upward from the particular fact to the general law; the man of affairs likewise guides himself by no *a priori* theory of how things must be, but by scrutiny of the actual course of events.   Why not make the experiment of treating religious experience in the same way?   Waiving all prophecies as to the results of this method, why should we not push it to the uttermost in order to secure all the advantages that lie within it, and the sooner to discover its limitations?

Postponing to a later chapter the questions that naturally arise at this point concerning the theoretical aspects of such a method of investigation, let us notice how this attitude of mind may be expected to affect our every-day religion. Here, it seems to me, the need for the new attitude is most pressing. For if there be a God, we ought to find him by some method more accessible to the common man than speculation can be. It would be suffocating to practical religion to make God's presence an inference rather than an experi-ence, to think that he should have spoken to men in the past but be silent now, or that he should talk to us through documents or proxies without responding to our own advances. What the hungry heart of our time needs is experience of an original, present relation to divine things. It is tired of going up into the heaven of speculation to bring God down, and into the depths of natural science to bring him up; that seems like going afar in search of our own fireside. Now, it is a daring thing to say to men of the modern type that God is very near them, even in their mouth and in their heart. A false religion cannot live by the experience of it, but only by misleading the intellect. An imperfect religion will have its imperfections speedily exposed when men bring it to the test of life. But a religion of experience, if such be possible, would be a no less glorious vindication of the truth than exposure of error. And so the question of assuming an empirical attitude of mind toward religion is the question of how vigorous our faith is. Is God the God of the living or of the dead? In any case, apart from all our planning, more and more the logic of the situation forces us toward a point where the authority of religion will depend upon its ability to produce what may be called a self-certifying life, a form of consciousness that needs not to go beyond itself to find its reason for existing, because it has within itself something of the Ultimate and the Eternal.

## The Scientific Standpoint is the Truly Conservative One.

This communion with God, or what appears to be such, in its various forms and degrees of development, constitutes the imperishable factor of all religion. Its best literary expression is sacred song. Hymns are longer lived than theological beliefs because they are the more direct and spontaneous expression of experience. They are but one degree removed from the concrete fact. The creed of the psalm-writers is long out of date, yet the song, "Lord, thou hast been our dwelling-place in all generations," is as fresh to-day as when it first broke from human lips. What the world most needs to-day is what it has always needed most, the experiences out of which song arises. And the empirical standpoint is the one from which men listen for the song.

This is the truly conservative standpoint. For experience, whether religious or other, is relatively abiding, while our reasonings about it are relatively shifting. While theories about light spring up and wither, the sun goes on warming and cheering. While literary men dispute about the authorship of the Iliad, the imperishable treasures of the great epic abide. Though philosophers cannot agree on the theory of ethics, conscience and moral ideals postpone nothing of their self-evidencing authority. Moral ideals do, indeed, undergo such changes as development implies, but they grow from within rather than by accretion from without. We grasp a higher ideal by devotion to the best we know. So, though religious experience be not stationary, it is relatively abiding; it is the original, vital fact, of which formulated beliefs attempt to give the description and explanation. Further, the experience develops from within, while the doctrine, in the nature of the case, is continuously affected by the changes in every branch of human learning. For this reason, the empirical attitude toward the facts of religious experience will lend stability to religious faith.

Religious bodies that place the emphasis of their practical work upon Christian experience ought to find less difficulty than they appear to in assimilating this way of thinking. These communions have said, substantially, "We know that God is present with us because we have experienced deliverance from sin, communion with his Spirit, and help in the struggles of life." The departure from the traditional standpoint of theology is here as real as it is unconscious. The logical affinity of such declarations is for the scientific and not for the scholastic method. Failure to realize this affinity is threatening to take away from these churches a great opportunity. Their logic of religious experience, almost unknown to themselves, is thoroughly modern. Practically applied, it would furnish a leverage precisely appropriate to a scientific age. Yet we behold mutual distrust between the propaganda of religious experience and the better elements of the modern spirit. One reason is not far to seek. There has been an attempt to serve two masters. When men have been invited to taste and see, the whole world has known that the "Thou must" of scholastic method lies concealed in the "Try it" of the modern invitation. Religious experience, which logically supplants dogmatism, has been pressed into the service of dogmatism. The facts of life have not been expressed in the natural language of modern men, but in the technical terminology of theological systems. The test of life has been only partially drawn from life itself, the silent assumption always being present that the experience must conform to a preconceived idea deduced from theological premises. If the churches would have their normal influence upon the modern world, let them work the idea of religious experience whole-heartedly! The future belongs neither to dogmatism nor to mere ethical culture, but to a religion of experience which will know how to be conscious of God without compromising the approved methods of studying facts.

The empirical attitude toward the facts of religion is in the closest relation to the accepted view of the immanence of God, just as, on the other hand, the dogmatic attitude is more nearly allied to the deism and quasi-deism that teach that God can be demonstrated but not experienced. If God is as fully present here and now as at any time and in any place, if the real environment of every soul is very God, the things we see and handle being modes of his self-expression, then observation and analysis are the most natural method of seeking for a sound interpretation of the universe and of life.

How much simplicity, courage, aggressiveness would religious thought gain from such a standpoint! Instead of assuming to be an outsider with respect to the other intellectual interests of men, it would assume that all thought constitutes one indivisible body. Religion would become a partner in every intellectual concern. Religion and science would not become one, nor would religious thought and natural science be fused; division of labor will always be necessary for minds of our limited range; but the difference of the tasks would not obscure as at present the affinity of spirit. The analytic method would be carried into daily living without detriment to spirituality, and conversely the sense of God would make of scientific investigation itself a kind of worship. Religious thought would not be a thing apart. It would not ask or accept release from the strictest principles of procedure. Presented with problems and difficulties, it would not demur to the jurisdiction of the court; rather, it would turn prosecutor and press the case to the utmost. Not by declining the canons of modern thought, in short, but by working them to the extent of their capacity, is religious thought to adjust itself to the modern world.

This method would undoubtedly reduce the number of confident assertions made in the name of religion. But so does winnowing grain reduce its bulk, and cutting a diamond lessen its size. Formulas hallowed by the lips and the hearts of generations of saints may cease to be repeated. Certainly a truer reverence will restrain the glibness with which men have talked of holy mysteries. And how precious will be the things of which we can say, "This I know!" As the content of our faith grows simpler, it becomes more obvious, more imperative, more real. Though the believer admits his uncertainty concerning many things that he would like to know, great is his peace concerning the things that remain. With regard to them, nothing can make him stumble. They comfort, and they command. His religion becomes simple, and it becomes intense. It is more ready than ever to take the aggressive, for, unencumbered with vast impedimenta needing constant defending, it goes directly at whatever needs to be done.

The church has not yet attained this high level of faith. She is still too keenly conscious of the contrast of past and present. But already the trembling and the shrinking are being allayed, and through tears she gathers hope, and some day hope will grow into the faith that is the victory over the world.

# AUTHORITY IN RELIGION

# CHAPTER III

## AUTHORITY IN RELIGION

Two classes of obstacles always stand in the way of the Christian religion: On the one hand, common faults of humanity, such as selfishness, war against the Christ in every age and in every man; on the other hand, there are hindrances peculiar to an age, a people, or a stage of culture. These do not necessarily indicate evil propensities. They may arise through misunderstanding, through the inertia of outgrown ideas and institutions, or through any incident that conceals the adaptation of Christianity to the needs of all men.

### *The Characteristic Obstacle of Our Age.*

Of these incidental obstacles, the one most characteristic of our age is the authoritative form assumed by official Christianity. During the last hundred years and more, politics and science have graven the notion of freedom ever deeper and deeper in the minds of men.

The individual no longer consents to be the passive terminus of ideas and of civil powers that originate above him. Government is not to be imposed upon the people, but is to be their own free expression of themselves. Similarly, science does not settle questions for men. It consists, rather, of the observations and inferences of many men clubbed together into a common fund upon which any man can draw at will, and which any one is at liberty to enlarge by new observations or more accurate inferences. In its own way, science is a republic—a republic of research.

Rightly or wrongly, there is a somewhat general feeling among intelligent men that Christianity, at least in its official garb, grants no corresponding freedom. In the other factors of civilization the individual is a source, but in religion he feels that he is required to be a mere point of application for something that takes its start outside him. He has no initiative, he can only comply. If he ventures to think outside the limits which he believes are set for him by the church, he suffers a sense of alienation from his fellows, and feels that he must classify himself with heretics and unbelievers. Men are assuming, for apparently trivial causes, that they are Ishmaelites in religious thought; and the reason of it, at least in part, is the astonishing ease with which many persons, under the impression that they are keeping the faith, treat as an enemy any individual who wanders from the herd.

We may, if we will, blame the spirit of the age for its opposition to authority; or we may blame the church for asserting authority; or we may divide the blame between the church and the world. But, wherever the fault lies, the fact remains to plague us. Practical values are being lost. Men stand aloof from the institutions of religion because of this real or supposed denial of freedom. That such men will ever be won to the church under present conditions, there is no reason to believe; nor on the other hand, is it as clear as it ought to be that the church intends to deal with these men in an open and fundamental manner.

*Attempted Solutions of the Difficulty.*

Three ways of meeting this difficulty have been attempted. The first is squarely to assert authority, and then to endeavor to enforce compliance. This is the solution of the problem of authority offered by the Roman Church. Absolutism is of the essence of Roman Christianity. The present has no appeal from the entail of tradition, the individual no appeal from the pope. In both faith and morals one can only submit.

Undoubtedly spiritual absolutism has attractions for some thinking men and for some moods. Freedom, because it requires initiative, can become a burden; and conversely, voluntary submission can imitate freedom by diminishing the sense of restraint. But the typical modern man, who prefers self-expression to repose, will not accept such a release; nor will it satisfy men who feel that moral and intellectual responsibility is something immediate to the individual, something that he cannot abdicate, even if he would.

A second proposed solution is implied in some Protestant teaching. It advises us that, after we have once submitted, we shall be so transformed that what is at first a sort of compulsion will become a free expression of our new self. This proposal admits the final value of free personality, and makes submission only a means thereto. It suffers, however, from the defect of affirming and denying at the same time. It asks me, in the name of my freedom, to become, for the time being, a mere terminus for an authority that, whatever it may be to others, is external to me. The thing is self-contradictory. If I do not for myself, and not merely through the persuasion of hearsay, perceive that what is demanded is reasonable and right, I abdicate my freedom if I submit. If you ask me to take your word as to the effects of submission, the reply is that, if free self-expression is of final worth, then my present self has the same right to expression as yours. On the basis of freedom and personal responsibility we cannot trade standpoints. My self-integrity demands that nothing move me to belief or to action that does not approve itself from the standpoint of my present knowledge and of my present sense of what is fitting and right.

The third alternative, and the only one left, is to accept the point of view of freedom, and then to show that the demands of the Christ and of our free personality coincide. According to this view, the Christ comes to me not as restraint, but as reinforcement of the inner liberty that marks the modern spirit. He asks me to accept nothing but what is approved by my present self. The acts that he commands can be seen to be required by my own moral standard. The doctrines that he expects me to believe can be reached by orderly procedure from what I already admit to be true. At no point does he require a break with what I am willing to own as my real self. Somewhere in my interviews with him I may discover that I have played the fool by taking for my real self some caricature of it, but yet, at whatever level of foolishness he finds me, he proceeds by unfolding something that is already there.

This conception of Christianity is no novelty. It has been implicit in theology from the beginning; for what is theology, as a whole, but an attempt to show that there is no break between what we are as rational beings, freely weighing evidence, and what we are as Christian believers? In proportion as theology proves anything it removes the occasion for invoking authority. Similarly, freedom rather than authority has been the assumption of practical preaching. The gospel preaches to the needs of men, to needs that men can be conscious of.  The really practical evangelism of the church is as far from repressing individuality as is an invitation to dinner.  One of the church fathers asserted that "the soul is naturally Christian," and biblical expression of this principle was found in the description of the Logos as the light that "lighteth every man."  When the Word comes to men, he comes to "his own."  Now, if I am "his own," even before I have welcomed him, then, in a true sense, he is already my own, so that I may appropriate him from the standpoint of what I now am.  He will not come down upon me as an external authority, but he will be found springing up within me as the life of my life, the self of my self.  In that case, all is freedom, and free self-expression merely blossoms when one is able to say, "I live, yet not I, but Christ liveth in me."

Doubtless this sounds natural, for it is what preachers have said to us again and again.  But the connection between such preaching and the question of authority in religion has not been made clear.  The preacher invites us to be our whole selves, asserting that then we must be Christ's, but we cannot help suspecting that somewhere in his program, or in the program of his church, there is the "either-or" of authority which forbids freedom. We need not scent insincerity in this preaching, but we may reasonably demand that the logical grounds of such a gospel be frankly canvassed and openly proclaimed.

We shall not go far in such a canvass before we discover that there is more than one kind of authority, and that authority of some kind religion does and must claim. There is, to be sure, a sort of *laissez faire* sentimentality that denies this. It tells us that one man's beliefs are as good as another's; that any man's religion is good enough for him; that active propagation of any religion is an impertinence; and that sending missionaries to China is just ground for irritation on the part of the Chinese empire, and constitutes a material palliation of the outrages of the Boxers. To the holders of this view, all religions look substantially alike, and so, upon us who are emphatic with our religion, there is shed a bland patronage, which tolerates while it pities.

But this is not the view of the average man of intelligence. He takes religion and religious differences seriously. He is sure that religion in general is not a blunder, and that, in some form, though he may be uncertain which one, it has a right to command us and to rouse us to intense earnestness. The world admires a man who is in "dead earnest" with the idea of God. Why? Because in positiveness, authoritativeness, it finds one mark of true religion.

Paradoxical as the statement is, what this age of freedom most wants to see is a religion that speaks with authority. A religion that barks at your heels you feel like kicking. One that says, "Won't you?" and, "Please do!" you turn away from as you do from the cant of professional beggary. But a religion that says, "Thou shalt!" makes you halt to see whether the reality of life hath not spoken in your ears. Once in a while a religious imposter assumes this tone, and the people flock about him for a time as though he were a prophet of the Almighty. You wonder how the populace can be misled by such impudent fraud, not noticing that the very audacity of the imposture gives it its greatest similitude to the truth.

The pulpit of to-day assumes not too much

authority, but too little. Rather, to speak precisely, it clings to a kind of authority that is discredited, and is timid or unclear in its assertion of another kind which strong men are ready to respect. They are not greatly impressed by defenses of the Christian system; they do not wish to be approached by the indirections of diplomacy; they will not be coaxed. But they will listen if their preacher will only speak with authority, and not as the scribes.

What, then, is this authority of which we have too much, and what is this other authority of which we have less than enough? The answer, in general, is, that there has been too much effort to coerce men by what they feel to be foreign to themselves, and that there has been too little of the imperative of conscience, and too little direct appeal to the instinctive needs of humanity. We have had too much compulsion, and not enough impulsion.

### Anomalies of the Protestant Attitude Toward Authority.

The appeal to authority as made by Protestants has generally taken the following form: You must believe this, and do that,

because God says so in the Bible. To
say that this is the imperialism of the
Roman Church over again, with a book
substituted for the pope, or that it contradicts
the Reformation principle of the soul's privilege of immediate approach to God, is merely
to repeat what has been many times shown.
The Reformation came up out of the hearts
of the people as their assertion, among other
things, of the rights of free personality. But
it knew not how to formulate and secure these
rights. It could not separate itself from the
inherited notion of God as monarch, and of
ourselves as passive subjects of his authority.
Religion continued to be thought of as coming down upon us rather than as springing up
within us. It was a law *for* life, but not a
law *of* life. Men continued to think of themselves as servants of God rather than as
friends of God. A really free attitude toward
the Scriptures was identified with impiety, and
the Bible of Protestantism became a store-
house of the thunders of authority.

It was natural that the church should
regard itself as a chosen instrument for giving
effect to the written word. It proceeded,
therefore, to construct authoritative statements

of what the Bible means. It formulated and worked into reasoned systems what the Bible does not formulate or even mention. It fixed upon the points where the lightnings of the Almighty should strike. Nations, churches, and individuals were classified and divided as the sheep are separated from the goats. Thus, divine authority, already translated into biblical authority, became further transformed into ecclesiastical authority. Every one knows the result, how the thunders of Jove dwindled into shillalahs in the hands of quarrelsome factions.

The Protestantism of to-day has largely receded from this last step—the identification of divine authority with that of the church— but it vacillates over the relation of divine authority to the Bible. It neither enforces authority unequivocally, nor unequivocally revises the notion of it. It does not command, but rather beseeches, that we hold fast to the tradition. As though genuine divine authority could ever need to beg or to debate! When a church descends to persuasion or to controversy on the point of authority, two things are likely to happen: First, men feel, if they do not infer, that the church has a weak case. It wishes to command as a superior, yet it argues as an equal. Second, to bolster up its case, the church assumes authority for its own reasonings about authority. Dogmatism declares, "Drink of the water of life from my cup or you shall not drink it at all," and so the old circle is completed again—divine authority, biblical authority, ecclesiastical authority. Face the conclusion, however, and it shrinks from your gaze, and thus the whole conception becomes shifty and ineffective. On the one hand, it advances, in theory, step by step from the authority of God to that of the Bible, and finally to that of the church doctrine. But in practice it retires step by step from authoritative doctrine to authoritative Bible, and thence to the authority of God.

That this last step in the regress is as necessary as the first, has become plain through study of the Bible itself. When men asked, "How do we know that the Scriptures are the very voice of God?" the answer was an attempt to prove the fact. Thus, the claims of the Bible were made dependent upon our reasonings about it, and authority actually got its own title from reason. This gave reason an exalted place, and the result was a strange blending of two kinds of compulsion. I say compulsion advisedly, for as soon as the authority of the whole divine scheme appeared to be staked upon logical grounds, theology felt obliged to give irresistible reasons. Theology thus came to have a double character. On the one hand, it cultivated the logical reason to an extreme point; and on the other, insisted on an authority above reason.

The logical objections to this procedure need not here be stated. But the practical effect of applying it must be noted, particularly with respect to the specific contents of the Bible. These were gotten at indirectly. First, logical grounds were offered to prove the authority of the Bible as a whole; next, the Bible was searched in order to find out just what it says; finally, its statements were affirmed to be true because they are parts of the authoritative whole. Thus, reason was granted the extraordinary capacity of discovering that the Bible is true before knowing what it contains; yet, in the same breath was asserted reason's extraordinary incapacity of dealing with the detailed contents on their own account. Reason could say that the whole Bible is true, but it could not apply the ordinary tests of accuracy to a single statement of fact contained therein. John Henry Newman applied this method with consistency when he said that the proper use of the private judgment is to find an authoritative teacher. No wonder that, as Bruce declares, the very word authority, "as employed in the sphere of religion, has become an offense to the friends of truth and freedom."

This blowing hot and blowing cold has made the Bible unreal to the intellect of our time. For it has necessitated modes of interpretation possible only to the unthinking and to those who are trained in doctrinal acrobatics. Precisely what is this Scripture to which authority is attributed? Is it the manuscripts in our possession, or the original manuscripts, whose precise contents we know nothing about? If the latter, authority fades away into the haze of an inaccessible past. On the other hand, if authority belongs to the documents as we know them, we are under the embarrassing necessity of reconciling all their doubtful points with our undoubted knowledge. If we find apparent errors in the authoritative words, we must show that they are not errors. This task is prescribed to us by our doctrine of scriptural authority. We have no alternative but to fit the facts to our pre-established theory. We are in the predicament of the boy who declared that "he must get the woodchuck, because the minister was coming to dinner, and there wasn't any meat in the house!" The theory simply has to drag out of the facts what has been promised. Hence the devices that I have already called acrobatics. Interpretation becomes a wriggling movement. It disposes of troublesome texts by supposing that the original words have been corrupted, or that some clew to the original meaning has been lost, or that somehow the passage doesn't mean just what it would mean if it were found outside of authoritative Scripture. The fact must be so because the authority of the book requires it to be so. The only difficulty consists in finding the right interpretation, and the "right interpretation" is, of course, the one that accords with the presupposition.

This is the unconscious sophistry that underlies such assertions as that "no established fact of science will ever contradict a properly interpreted statement of the Bible." Of course not, for to be "properly interpreted'' means to be interpreted in such a way as not to contradict any established fact of science! Any other interpretation would be improper because it would wreck the presupposition. Thus facts push the interpretation hither and thither. The Bible becomes a variable element. It becomes less and less a definite reality in men's thoughts, and yet this very wabbling movement is supposed to constitute a defense of its unchanging authority.

If it be said that this description does not apply to the biblical scholarship of the present day, we may gladly admit the fact. Certainly the thought of our day is casting aside this ragged coat which Protestantism inherited from Rome. The investigator, in his own mind, is already free. He goes at the fact unencumbered by assumptions as to what he must find there. It is true, also, that fagot and stake do not await him at the end of the road. Yet excommunication as a penalty for scholarship is only now becoming impossible, and there are still possible ecclesiastical censure, deprivation of office, oral denunciation, and pursuit by a blood-hound press. As Lowell says:

" Fagot and stake were desperately sincere:
    Our cooler martyrdoms are done in types."

Further, though the professional scholar is
free in his own mind, the fruits of such freedom have not been made available to the
people.   There is a chasm between what the
scholar knows and what the people are officially taught, or at least allowed to believe.
Outgrown views of Scripture are constantly
assumed and appealed to in the ministrations
of the clergy.   Not in the scholar's study,
but in the daily life of the world is the picture
of authority which I have sketched a menacing
reality.   For something of the new biblical
learning has come to the ears of the common
people.   Once in a while a preacher explains
and approves it; more often the pulpit condemns it or assumes to defend the Bible
against it; most often of all, perhaps, the
newspaper gives a distorted glimpse of it.
Thus the public has become aware that a new
view of the Bible, entertained by men of learning, contradicts the view usually taught or
assumed in the churches.   Passive minds and
minds that have acquired their permanent
"set" suffer little personal inconvenience
from this fact, but active minds and minds in

process of formation feel a strain between the old and the new. In the interest of such minds, the standpoint of freedom should be frankly adopted in popular instruction, and there should be no blinking of the defects of the outworn method.

Something of this kind must be done soon, or we shall be in the scandalous fault of believing one thing and teaching another. The church can survive many and grievous mistakes honestly made, but she must be above the suspicion of insincerity. Within Protestantism, too, there cannot be one doctrine for priest and another for people. Our reason for existing as Protestants is the right of the believer to direct access to the Scriptures, and to whatever concerns his spiritual life. This implies a teaching function which Protestantism is fulfilling in only equivocal fashion. For certainly the scholarship of the churches has decided that scientific method in the study of the Bible is a sound method. The day for hoping to crush it is well behind us. Literary and historical criticism, as a method, is here to stay. Its present product may be revised to any degree; its procedure in special problems may be improved; but the right to raise its questions, and the right to solve them as other similar problems are solved, have been won forever. Now, this necessitates a reconstruction of the basis of biblical teaching in the church. We cannot combine the new scholarship and the old method of instruction, nor can the two exist side by side. They cannot exist side by side, because of the genius of Protestantism and because of modern methods of diffusing knowledge. They cannot be combined because they are opposed to each other. Authority, to exist at all, must be adequate; and if it is adequate to all the details included under it, there is no room for scientific method. Conversely, if scientific method be of service at any one point, a new principle is admitted which requires us to revise our notion of authority all along the line.

Instead of coming at the details of the Bible from a theory of what the Bible is as a whole, then, we must first examine the contents part by part, and from them infer the nature of the whole. This merely applies to the parts the same rational faculties that the older apologetics applied to the whole, but just here lies the kernel of the question. Under the new assumption, the Bible is just what its contents are found to be by scrutiny thereof in the light of literary and historical science and of our experience of spiritual things. Its authority is that of a body of ascertained facts. Any statement becomes credible, not through a belief that it must be true because it is in the Bible, but either because its origin and setting make it trustworthy, or because the substance of what it asserts can be tested by us in our daily living. We shall believe that there was such a man as John the Baptist, on the historical evidence of the fact, and we shall believe that we ought to love our neighbor as ourself because the principle of love approves itself directly to our conscience and to our experience of life. On the other hand, we shall not be troubled if Kings and Chronicles, or Matthew and Luke disagree; and if the imprecatory psalms are heathenish we shall not apologize for them. We shall go at the facts unencumbered by assumptions as to what we must find there. We may even dispense with the true but misused distinction between two kinds of higher criticism, one destructive the other not so. This distinction lends itself all too easily to the notion that some biblical studies are to be approved because their results do not jar our nerves, while others are to be condemned because they disturb our presuppositions. There is no touchstone for discriminating good criticism from bad except that one accords with facts, while the other does not.

## Reconstruction of the Notion of Authority.

But, it may be asked, is the Bible on exactly the same level as any other book? Has it no unique authority? Is everything reduced to a religious go-as-you-please? For the old-fashioned "Thus saith the Lord" must we substitute "Thus saith higher criticism"? If so, with the coming of modern methods,

" There hath past away a glory from the earth,"

and one might almost wish that time would turn backward and make us intellectual children again, in order that we might hear once more the thunders of Jehovah in the written word.

If the church is called to deal frankly with the people by leading them up to the new points of view, emancipated intellect has the converse duty of showing how, in view of the

new learning, spiritual values are to be con-
served. How shall the people realize that
God has spoken comfort to their hearts and
commands to their wills? There was a time
when a plain man would go to the Bible to
settle questions of belief or of conduct.
When he found a passage that seemed to fit
his case, he simply appropriated it, in the firm
conviction that God had uttered it in order to
solve just such difficulties. The sorrowing
heart also and the sin-laden conscience went
straight to the written word and there they
heard the wondrous consolations of God. We
must deal soberly with facts like these. To
be sure, they do not alter the demands of
sound method in Bible teaching, but they do
cry aloud for a divine authority on which men
can lean. The plain man knows that he is
not sufficient to himself. He wants to hear
the voice of God, and he wants to hear it in
no uncertain tones. What can we say to
him?

We can at least deal openly with his difficulty, and that will be worth something.
Dissent is twin brother to distrust, and eva-
sion of issues is their mother. If the church
is to inherit the world, she will have to be

meek in her intellectual as well as her other attitudes. Meeting the inquirer in this spirit, we can say that the notion of authority is undergoing a change. Admitting that this change is a profound one, we may point out that it involves no new or revolutionary idea, but only the development of ideas that have been present in Christianity from the beginning. It does not put God out of the Bible, or weaken the notion of revelation, but rather brings the revelation more near to us. The book has been to us what the temple was to the Jews, the very dwelling-place of God. Yet has our use of the sacred writings concealed him, as did the temple. For when an inquiring mind has asked whether this or that word is the very word of God, we have had to interject an "if." This is the word of the Highest if our doctrine of scriptural authority is correct. Thus, to many minds, a partition wall built by human hands shuts off the direct vision of God. The new view of authority removes this partition. Let us see how this is done.

How the nerves of scribe and of Pharisee must have been shocked by Jesus' method of acquainting the people with divine things!

He merely declared what he regarded as truth, omitting to say why we should believe it. The compulsion of argument and the compulsion of scriptural authority are both lacking. The official teachers began everything with an "It is written," and then followed elaborate expositions, and the reason for believing the exposition was always the theory of an authoritative written revelation. Jesus simply ignored this whole method. He did not need it for himself, and what is more remarkable, he took for granted that his hearers did not need it. For him and for them alike there was access to the holiest place of divine truth. One would have difficulty to find more complete emancipation from authority than he represents in his own person. And what he was he wished his disciples to be. As the Father was in him, so he himself was to be in them, and the Spirit of Truth, not tradition or mere logic, was to guide into all truth. In point of method, then, Jesus made as complete a break with scriptural authority as could well be.

If we should stop here, however, the picture would be incomplete. For it was noted by observers that, though Jesus did not teach as did the scribes, nevertheless he did teach with authority. He freed himself from one type of authority, yet he puts before us the supreme example of another, more compelling type. The self-assurance with which he declared the things of God would be ridiculous if it were not sublime, and it is sublime because his words carry immediate conviction to the heart and conscience. As the eternal hills need no buttresses to hold them up, so the words of the Great Teacher lean not upon the past or upon any syllogism, but are self-supporting.

Again, though Jesus broke with the method of Jewish tradition, he did not disconnect himself from its contents. He came not to destroy, but to bring to fulness. He recognized God's presence in the history of his people; he personally observed the ordinances of the law; he accommodated his teaching to his hearers. His method was not that of lawless destruction, but rather the method of life, which brings forth the better by unfolding the possibilities of the inferior. To cite a single example, is it not striking that the most complete statement of the Christian principle of life, the double law of love, is put forth as an interpretation of the law and the prophets, and not as something new?

The reorganization in the thought of authority that is now taking place is an effort to assimilate the method of Jesus. It is an aspiration after the attitude of freedom that he expected in his immediate disciples. We are to assert for ourselves as much liberty as he assumed for them, and we are to recognize the authority to which he bowed.

What positive content, then, abides in the notion of authority in religion? First, there is a rightful authority of history and of testimony. Though we must weigh all things for ourselves, we must not set ourselves apart from the historical process. We are part of a great order of development, and only a part. Each generation has a right, of the same kind as our own, to its place in this order. Both the good and the bad at any stage of progress are linked to what went before and to what comes after. It is never possible for us to "quit and begin all over again." Revising the calendar, and calling our day the "year one" is as vain in religion as it was in French politics.

One aspect of authority, then, is identical with the historical sense. It assumes that anything that has taken strong hold of men has some reason for existing—a reason that has some positive relation to our own life and times. There was good reason why strong monarchies should spring up as the successors of feudalism, and that reason, formulated into a principle, is a part of our own political science. So the doctrines of the church are the language of something that lies deep down in human nature.

With one's first taste of intellectual independence, one is apt to fancy that the old world is a crude affair, which young men like one's self must make over before it will amount to much. Such self-projection is natural to the young man's stage of growth. He himself is passing out of a child's world into a man's world, and the subjective experience is so absorbing as to color all he sees. He beholds two worlds, an old one and a new one, and the whole meaning of things appears to be that the old should give place to the new. The world must move with him. If it does not, he is vexed. He frets at the apparent immobility of thought; he chafes at the indifference of men to his youthful vision. His visions are not false, but they contain only a part of the spectral colors. To see things in the white light of truth, he must acquire the historical sense. He must learn that he himself, with his ideals, is a product of this old world. Incomplete as it is, too, this world is made up of the stratified ideals of other young men who, in the vast succession of the generations, have struggled for a future better than their own present. Thus ideas and institutions are ever old and young at the same time. Authority and individualism are inseparable. Authority is the individualism of the past, and individualism is an effort to make authority of the present. Choose one to the exclusion of the other, and you tie yourself to the merely temporal. What we need is to discern the eternal in the process of the ages, and the effort so to do is true allegiance to authority.

The authority of testimony is the same thing seen from another angle. Beliefs are never creations of mere thought. From the rudest pagan idea of God to the most elaborate "plan of salvation," doctrine has a real relation to experience. Rarely, if ever, is that relation one of arbitrary symbolism, for there is a reason why one symbol is preferred to another. Hence the deposit of religious tradition comes to us as an index, however partial, of the experiences of humanity. The vitality of Christian dogma is due to its relation to the unquenchable life of the spirit. It outlives its own defective logic because it does not live by that kind of bread alone. It is an outward sign of an inward experience. Generation after generation, a mighty power has gripped men, and the system of doctrine is a stammering effort to testify to it. The theory of biblical infallibility and authority is itself a memorial of the irresistible conviction with which the Scriptures have found men out and influenced their hopes and fears and conduct.

In our reconstruction of the idea of authority, therefore, we are not to destroy, but to bring to fulness. Just as Jesus, though freeing himself from the trammels of ancient logic, nevertheless recognized his organic relation to the whole past of his people, so our task is not merely to reject an inadequate and mischievous theory of authority, but also to bring to fuller growth the spiritual germ out of which the notion of authority grew.

In the second place, not only must we recognize the rightful authority of history and of tradition, but we must also experience and proclaim the present authority of spiritual things. In this, also, we must be like Jesus. We must share in his consciousness of a divine kingdom as the reality of our life and of all worlds. No man was ever more spontaneous in his mental attitudes than Jesus, yet no one could be less arbitrary. Though he be the most commanding figure in history, yet even he finds life in no individualism, but only by merging himself into that ultimate community of life in which men share in the life of God, and God shares in the life of men, and each man in the life of his fellows. He found life just as he tells us we may find it, by losing all the arbitrariness and egoism out of it.

The spiritual authority to which he bowed is binding upon us. In its least developed form, it is the consciousness of duty as contrasted with inclination. In this form it is a burden imposed upon one, a compulsion that seems to come from without. But at a higher stage of moral development we discover that duty is not imposed upon us, but expresses our very self. When the habit of obedience is well formed, too, we think less and less of duty, and more and more of moral ideals, of something that is worth striving and even suffering for. We dream dreams of a golden age that is to be, and we find happiness in laboring for its realization. We are now free, and yet we are under authority, for these visions hold us in willing captivity. What ought to be has become a passion to which we are ready to sacrifice what is.

Thus authority meets us at the outset of our moral existence, grows with our growth, and is most effective when we are most free. Now, this authority, already recognized in conscience and moral ideals, is one with the authority of religion. Not that religion is to be reduced to morals, but that morals, considered as regulating relations between man and man, are to be looked upon as parts or aspects of a regulative whole which contains the total meaning of life. In religion, as in morals, the higher self commands us. What would be impels what is; what should be uses the world that is as plastic material out of which to shape forth the eternal truth. The world as mere fact is but half real. It is a body waiting for the breath of life, waiting for power to obey, to hope, to love, to sacrifice, and to have faith that ideals contain the truth of things.

Religion is no more an invention than is sleeping or breathing. It does not come to us through reasoning. It does not wait even for our deliberate volition. It is a spontaneous outgoing of the eternal hope, the eternal preference for ideals, that make us men and not beasts. To ask whether religion has authority, is the same as asking whether ideals have a right to mold us and the things about us into their own likeness.

When this question is answered in the affirmative, then the authority of Christianity is seen to depend upon the adequacy of Jesus' interpretation of the ideal side of our nature. If his commands conflict with what we most deeply are; if, in coming to him, we do not come to our very selves; then, indeed, he has not authority over us. But, as a matter of fact, his influence over men is a living demonstration of his authority. He says, "Do this," and our own conscience echoes, "Do it!" He speaks of God as our Father, and our hearts leap to hear him. He tells us of the laws of spiritual life and growth, and our ex-

perience confirms his words. He declares a
future in which what ought to be shall be,
and something within us responds that it must
be so.

All this he does without a word of argument. This is authority in religion, then, but
not authority in theology. Theology is a
structure built by reason. Its conclusions
stand upon premises. If the premises are
good, and the inferences are logically drawn,
it needs no further authority. If the premises are not good, or the inferences are falla-
cious, no authority can make good the defect.
The science of divine things has the same
kind of authority as any other science,
namely, that of correct observation and of
logical inference. From no other source
could its propositions derive a right to command us. But the authority of religion is
more and different. It is not the compulsion
of a theory, however correct it may be, but
the impulsion of our whole higher self.

Authority in religion cannot be escaped.
It is not an invention, it is not a product of
thought, it is not a tradition—it is a law of
life. Edward Everett Hale, in his "Man
without a Country," tells the story of one

who renounced all the restraints of government. Being unable to put foot upon land, since all the land is under authority, he became a wanderer for life upon the unsocial sea, and thus his supposed freedom turned into galling bondage. He discovered that government is not imposed upon man, but is man. So religious authority, though we may not escape it, yet coincides with liberty. It is within us. It is what we are, demanding to express itself, to be fed, to grow. It is as natural and inevitable as our instincts, and what we call submission to it is nothing but self-expression in one of its highest forms.

SOME THINGS THAT WE KNOW; A
MEDITATION AT THE DOORWAY
OF THE NEW CENTURY

# CHAPTER IV

## SOME THINGS THAT WE KNOW; A MEDITATION AT THE DOORWAY OF THE NEW CENTURY

The growth of the American college during the latter half of the nineteenth century has developed in the American student a new attitude toward religion. Our system of higher education had its origin chiefly in a demand for educated clergymen, and to educate for the ministry was to hand down the treasures of the faith. A college was a place for mental training and for teaching what was already known. Its students were expected to take their religion as well as their information upon authority, and a doubting or questioning attitude was looked upon with disapproving apprehension.

But with the coming of university ideals into college life, a

*Spirit of Uncertainty*

has become common, if not general. The instructor still has the duty of imparting what is known, and in most places the truth of religion is still assumed, but the atmosphere is humid with the sweat of inquiring spirits. The function of the university is not only to conserve, but also to correct and extend human learning. Under the influence of its ideal, attention turns naturally to what is still in discussion and away from what is admitted to be true. Many a youth who enters college expecting that now the great problems of life will be settled for him has found out that a modern college is not a place where things are settled for men, but rather where the responsibility of settling things for one's self grows most acute.

Thus it comes to pass that the college student of to-day feels keenly the instability of human opinions and the difficulty of being sure of one's beliefs. He is tempted to feel that nothing abides, that nothing has really been settled. Particularly at the doorway of the new century, when all eyes turn to behold the mighty transformations of a brief hundred years, comes this sense of uncertainty. This, accordingly, is a favorable moment for turning aside from the things that we see in rapid movement to ask ourselves whether there be not something that abides from age to age. Is mankind totally at sea with respect to the weightiest interests of life, or are some things actually settled?

In a general way, the question almost answers itself. For, compared with the totality of our life, the part given up to speculative questionings is very slight indeed. Mankind as a whole does not stand trembling on the shore of life, hesitating to embark because it knows not the paths of the sea; on the contrary, we are already out on the deep, and nothing could convince us that we do not know whether we are making progress toward our desired haven. There are great certainties by which we live, and these far outweigh the uncertainties that remain. We are not forever getting ready to meet reality; we are wrestling with reality here and now. We know the chief things that one needs to learn in order to distinguish the true coin of life from its various counterfeits. By these certainties the college student lives even when he fancies that nothing is settled. Let him listen a moment, and he will hear the Yes and No of his real life. It is only because they have become so spontaneous, so fully identified with his very self, that he fails to realize that his whole life is in reality a great affirmation.

A simple, steady look within us and about us will reveal, among other things, four great assertions that we can safely make, which, taken in their totality, should go far toward calming the religious inquietude of any earnest soul. First,

*We Know that in Each of Us there is a Higher and a Lower Set of Tendencies.*

Competition is going on for the mastery of our life. You may call it, in theological terms, a struggle between Satan and the Spirit of God; or you may call it, in biological language, an effort to adjust ourselves to environment against unsocialized remnants of the ape and tiger nature. In any case, the contest is a fact that each of us knows for himself, irrespective of the catechism, and of all theories, whether biological or theological.

The fact of this internal contest awakens a thousand problems as to its origin, its function in the development of man, and its bearing upon the destiny of the individual and of the race. Into such questions let us not enter. They are secondary and less certain than the fact itself. The fact, whatever be its relations, we know. Some of our tendencies are higher than others, and when we call them higher, we mean that they ought to have the mastery of us. This "ought" might also awaken many legitimate and important problems, but we pass them all by in order to focus our attention upon the certainty of the fact with which we deal.

The rudimentary character of our proposition may easily obscure the proportions of the truth which it conveys. We can easily study man as a mere object, just as we study an egg or a microbe. We may observe the mechanism not only of his physical organism, but also of his mind. Under given conditions we look for a mental effect as well as for a physical resultant. Thus we may build up a science of the mind, every proposition of which states what is, while no word says what ought to be. We may even include in our science the fact that men feel a sense of ought and ought not, and we may theorize as to how this sense originated. The story of its origin is in turn merely a statement that something is, not that something is better than something else, or that the better ought to be preferred. Men sometimes fancy that they can describe the whole of human life in this manner. Yet we know not only that something is and that something has been, but also that something ought to be. From neither of these propositions is there any escape. We may say without hesitation that this is settled. Not only is our moral nature a fact; its fundamental deliverance and assumption are true.

If you ask for proof that something ought to be, I decline to answer, just as I would refuse to consider evidence that sunlight is more bright than candlelight. It is possible for you to desire that it were not so; it is possible to benumb the sense that it is so; but whosoever experiences the extinction of the consciousness of obligation becomes thereby as truly insane as one who becomes unable to distinguish the real from his own imaginings. This fact of the commanding authority of the higher over the lower, just because it needs no proof, is one of the things that the ebb and flow of opinion do not reach. The swinging doors of centuries and of millenniums will turn, and through the vast aisles of time learning will come and go with the changing genera-

tions, but every man will know this eternal
truth.

*We Know that, as far as these Higher Ten-
dencies Have to do with Our Relations to
our Fellows, Their Best Interpretation is
Found in the Law of Brotherly Love.*

The distinction usually made between morals and religion is, that the one has to do with
the relations of men to one another, while the
other concerns our relations to God. Without stopping to ask whether this distinction is
fundamental, we may say, without hesitation,
that at least the moral world is at the feet of
him who taught us to love our neighbor as
ourselves. Morally reflective men everywhere, in Christian and non-Christian coun-
tries alike, whether or not they are members
of the church or even worshipers of God, confess that Jesus was right in respect to at least
the second of the two great commandments.
Thus much of the content of duty we do not
guess at or speculate about—we know.

We need not now raise the question whether
this moral precept is exclusively Christian;
it may have been more or less clearly announced by Confucius, Gautama Buddha, or

the Hebrew prophets.  Possibly Jesus himself had no thought of making an innovation. The only essential point for us just now is, that we know that he was right.

To say how we know that he was right, would take us too far afield.  It is enough that, whatever difficulties we may have in the application of the principle, however great and apparently interminable may be the tangle of competing human interests, no one of us does, as a matter of fact, escape the conviction that brotherly love is a beautiful thing, and also our bounden duty.

This, in a nutshell, is the practical outcome of the whole ethical movement of the last generation.  Ethical philosophers differ among themselves on many points, but they agree that man is a social being, that all morality is social morality.  In the long run, the ethical movement amounts to this: that Jesus was right, and that we can discover reasons that show why he was right.

In a similar way, the various types of religion converge at this point.  All the warring sects of Christianity agree that we should love one another.  But not less certainly the great systems that compete with Christianity admit the truth of this part of our religion. Their argument runs: "We, too, inculcate the duty of brotherly love. We feed the hungry, and clothe the naked. Herein our religion is as good as yours!" Sometimes representatives of another religion lay claim to this virtue in a superior degree, as when they point out that they and their fellow religionists abstain from killing even inferior animals. It would be interesting to inquire how far the teaching of human brotherhood is indigenous in the non-Christian religions, and how far it really coincides in substance with the teachings of Jesus. Is the praise of brotherly love which we hear from our neighbors of India due to some inherent force in their religion, or has it been to some extent inspired by contact with Christian ideals? Into such questions we need not go, for this, at least, is certain: Whether through the historic influence of Jesus, or through other sources of divine illumination also, or even through the ordinary play of social forces, the non-Christian as well as the Christian world admits that Jesus was right when he commanded us to love one another.

The command to love one another was connected with a parallel command to love

God. When we ask whether this, also, is known to be a valid injunction, we are confronted with the fact that, whereas we can see and hear our fellowmen, we appear to have no parallel way of assuring ourselves that there is a God whom we can love, and from whom we may look for a loving response. Yet, in the strength of our moral convictions, we can at least assert that we know that,

*Whether or Not there is a Loving God, there Ought to be One.*

It was no mere accident that led Jesus to couple these commands together. We can conceive that he was deluded into the belief in the existence and in the loving kindness of God. But he was certainly not mistaken in his conception of what would constitute an ideal or even decent universe. In a world in which love is the law for men, there ought to be a loving God. This proposition rests on no merely philosophical considerations, but rather upon the conscious demands of our moral nature. Morality aims at completeness, wholeness; and love, which is the fulfilling of the law, defines that wholeness as the unity of personal communion. If the universe as a whole is without a heart, then love is cheated of its dues.

Consider what it means that the world has contained one such man as Jesus. Where will you find anything at once as complete and yet as fragmentary as his life? Complete in its devotion to ideal good, it was yet woefully fragmentary in its realization, or apparent realization, of good. With utter self-abandonment, Jesus gives himself to the promotion of an ideal society, which he calls the kingdom of God. This society is intended to embrace the whole world and all ages. Its bond of union is brotherly love; and confidence that love is not only a law for us, but also a law of the universe, yields a basis for faith in the perpetuity and universal triumph of the kingdom, and in its adequacy to rule the whole of our troubled existence.

Brotherly love is final for us provided it is thus final for the whole universe of which we are parts. The reasonableness of any moral principle rests upon its harmony with the nature of things as they are. Jesus lived his marvelous life wholly upon the supposition that love to fellowmen merely carries into our conduct the actual nature of things. You cannot separate these two—his attitude toward men and his faith in God—without destroying all that is characteristic in his personality. Fancy Jesus without faith in the fatherhood of God! At once there slips out of the picture his consciousness of ultimate unity upon which is built both the symmetry and the matchless goodness of his character. Not that he was good for the sake of rewards; that would have brought division into his character,—a part of his life being lived here, and a larger part there,—whereas the wondrous thing about him is his ability to be a complete man even in an incomplete world. He lived in the Ultimate; it was the reality in which he moved. And, just as he found the Ultimate, not apart from his life, but within it, so the ideal society which he founded was not, in his thought, a means to an end, but itself an end. It was to be God's own kingdom and dwelling-place, in which he is so present that one and the same set of acts on our part engenders at once an ideal relation between man and man and between man and God.

Suppose, now, that Jesus, filled with devotion to these ideal ends, was mistaken as to the existence or as to the fatherhood of God;

suppose that the inspiration, the sense of the Ultimate, that irradiates his whole being and makes a kingdom of God in the midst of our imperfect conditions seem practicable—suppose that this was illusory. What a shabby universe would it be! A universe that could produce such a man and then disappoint him would deserve the contempt of decent men! Let us say it boldly; if there be no loving God who is the source, the inspiration, and the crown of human brotherhood—if human love is nothing at all but froth upon the waves of an unfeeling world-process—then shame on the universe that has brought us forth!

Various schemes of thought have sought to show that we can get along even if there be no loving God. Enjoy yourself as you go along, says the Epicurean. Make no demands for yourself, and then you will not be disappointed, says the Stoic. But both these schemes are self-regarding; neither meets the problems arising under the assumption that brotherhood is a law of life. Provided I make my own interest the end of my existence, I can endure a Godless universe by fighting for myself, or, if need be, by extinguishing myself to escape the pains of existence. But the case is different when life becomes love rather than self-gratification. To love unselfishly is to make demands of a positive nature upon the universe; it is to assert the existence of values which I am not at liberty to surrender. Does the universe care, or does it not care, for those whom I regard as ends in themselves? I am not searching for incentives to beneficent conduct, but for respect for those whom I love. This is no question of rewards and punishments, but solely a question whether the universe has regard for beings who are worthy of it. It ought to have such regard. There ought to be a God who is our Father!

*We Know that Vast Numbers of Men Who have Applied in Practical Life the Hypothesis of a God, Who is Our Father, have Found their Belief in it Strengthened through Experience.*

We have not been born into an atheistic or even a doubting world, but into a world of religious faith. The great questions of life and destiny are not new. They have not been postponed in order that we might solve them. It would be the most foolish of youthful folly to forget that multitudes of our fellows, past and present, may have something to contribute out of their thought and experience. Above all, we must not lose sight of the fact that the hypothesis of the existence of God has already undergone a long and severe test.

Youth easily fancies that such high themes as God and immortality are to be approached solely by the road of deductive reasoning. Quite the contrary. A practical man trusts things more than thoughts, experience more than syllogisms. And these questions do not dwell merely in the air, apart from the business of life. We wish to know what sort of real world we are in contact with. The core of this question, accordingly, is not, "How much has been proved?" but rather, "What hypothesis best fits life as we experience it?"

Let us not misunderstand one another at this point. We are talking of verification of hypotheses, but verification takes many forms. If, for example, an anthropologist should form the hypothesis that a certain region is inhabited by a tribe of pygmies, the verification would consist in penetrating the region and exploring it with one's own eyes. If, on the other hand, the hypothesis be that the climate of this region is a favorable or unfavorable one for a certain class of persons, the verification would not be so simple. No one person's observation would suffice, but there would be needed the general impression of a considerable number of observers. Let us take another illustration of this difference. If we wish to know what the planet Mars is made of, we can find out by using the spectroscope. But if the question be whether Mars is inhabited, the test is very different. None of our instruments is powerful enough to reveal a Martian inhabitant directly to our eyes. Yet it is conceivable—its probability is another thing—that a long series of observations of changing phenomena upon the surface of Mars should ultimately yield a rationally firm conviction that we behold the work of intelligences like our own. Such verification would be genuine, though it should never show to our senses a single inhabitant. The hypothesis would be verified by demonstrating its accordance with a considerable body of growing experience.

In this sense it is possible to verify the hypothesis of the existence of God. If there be a God, then men who believe in him, and apply this belief in actual life, should be expected, on purely rational grounds, to grow more rather than less confident of such belief. But, if there be no God, belief in him would be gradually weakened, and finally destroyed, by the same process. For, just as far as we live at all, we are in intercourse with things as they are. Life involves interaction with environment. Therefore, the growing experience of the race, and the accumulated testimony of the Christian centuries, have a right to be heard when the question of God's existence or of his loving fatherhood is raised.

We know that nearly all men have entertained some sort of belief in God, and that, in some manner and in some degree, they have cumulatively brought their belief to the test of life. Similarly, multitudes, accepting Jesus' declaration of the loving character of God, have sought to live in its light and by means of its power. What is the resultant impression upon the generality of men? Does the hypothesis seem to work, or does it not?

Men's ideas of God have certainly changed, but in the main the changes have been for the better; that is, a heavier rather than lighter weight has been placed upon the God-idea. Here and there an individual, particularly those who demanded that God be manifested in some particular fact more than in the totality of life, has been disappointed. Yet, looking at the history of man as a whole, and at the history of Christianity in particular, we cannot fail to perceive that the God-idea has perennial vitality, or that the Christian form of this idea is an all-conquering one. Measuring the movements of thought, not by centuries, but by millenniums, we behold humanity in ever-greater numbers and in ever-increasing degree daring to trust that the center of things is a heart of sympathy. The world as a whole gives its testimony to the appropriateness of the hypothesis to the facts of life. Let us grant that we see as yet no way in which we can perfectly adjust the notion of the fatherhood of God to the facts of our imperfect and painful existence. Many things happen that, taken by themselves, would lend plausibility to the atheistic hypothesis. It is therefore all the more remarkable that atheism and despair have made so poor a showing in their contest with the theistic and Christian hypothesis. The experience of the world, as a whole, tends to show that Jesus' idea of God is the best interpreter of life we have as yet discovered. It leaves fewest dark corners, and adjusts, better than anything else has done, the practical machinery of life. Men who live as in the presence of God somehow find themselves increasingly possessed by a conviction that God is actually present as the most real factor of their environment, and even of their own being. Proofs are rarely asked for, and often they appear to be an impertinence. To most men the existence of God is as little in need of proof as the duty of loving kindness. The very atmosphere of life has divinity in it. This is more than the persistence of a tradition impressed upon us in childhood, for men outgrow the myth-making and myth-believing instinct in everything else, and even in religion. It is not a romantic dream of youth, for youth is the period of greatest doubt, and maturity the period of greatest faith. It is not a temperamental trait of feminine natures, or a mark of the undeveloped minds of ignorant masses, for the most masculine and the most creative minds of the race have, with comparatively few exceptions, been strong believers.

Our religious uncertainties are far less numerous and far less serious than we are

tempted, in a time like this, to suppose.
There is unshaken standing-ground for a religious and a Christian life outside of and above
all the battle-fields of opinion. The great fact
of duty stands out upon the human horizon as
boldly as Mont Blanc from the valley of Cha-
monix; and as the rising and the setting sun
illumines the everlasting snows upon the head
of this most glorious of the Alps, so Jesus'
principle of love to fellowmen gives content
and meaning to the moral imperative. Even
when we come to the mighty mysteries of ultimate being we are not left in darkness. For,
as our moral nature points out a pathway for
our feet upon the earth, it also looks upward
and dares to speak to the vast silence. If
our age cannot be certain that a sensible sign
has been given in response, if we must walk
by faith rather than by sight, even faith has
its own way of verifying itself. Though no
indubitable word come through the mists,
though no compelling vision scatter them,
nevertheless somehow, possibly through the
inspiring influence of Jesus, the moral nature
has gathered courage to assert the ultimate-
ness of its own authority by declaring, "It
must be so!" This is one of the practical

certainties by which we live. And the soul that lives by such practical certainties, loving fellowmen and venturing something of loving confidence toward him whom we have not seen, somehow finds the facts of existence falling into order, is comforted, and feels that it is not alone.

# MORAL FOUNDATIONS OF
## SPIRITUALITY

# CHAPTER V

## MORAL FOUNDATIONS OF
SPIRITUALITY

That religion has some vital bond of union with morals no one doubts. Possibly they are right who assert a mutually independent origin for morals and religion, but if so, religion adopted morals into itself at a very early stage of development. For us a religion that did not concern itself with right and wrong would be no religion at all.

The practical aspects of this relationship, however, have been looked for chiefly in only one of the two possible directions. Men have come at morals from the side of religion, saying truly that whoever is religious will be a doer of the right. Far less often is the question raised whether doing right has an essentially religious quality within itself. As far as my observation goes, goodness has been commonly represented as a necessary consequence of religion, rather than as itself a religious fact. It is said that if one is religious one

will *also* be good.   This is probably due, however, more to the persistence of a form of
expression than to any actual sympathy for
the old custom of placing religion and morality
in contrast with one another.

Nevertheless, the comparative neglect of
the second mode of approach, which looks for
the spiritual aspect of moral qualities, has left
us less fortified than we should be against
misunderstandings and internal dissensions.
In various directions and under various circumstances we suffer the consequences of

*Misplaced Emphasis.*

When, for example, questioning of fundamental beliefs becomes widespread and profound, there is a tendency to assume that the
doubt is more serious than it really is.   Because some things are being reweighed, men
fear that no values are secure.   Yet, all the
while, the moral foundations of the spiritual
life remain untouched.   It is most often the
intellect, most rarely the will, that is concerned
in the puzzles of life.   Unless we realize that
this is true, we may endure torments whenever the winds of doctrine shift, being afflicted
with a sort of spiritual rheumatism.

Again, when religion becomes so far organized as to be formal, to employ a technical vocabulary, and to assume a professional tone, then also men easily put other things into the place that belongs to moral principle. It is possible for moral decay to take place at the very time when one sincerely prides one's self upon one's fidelity to the faith that was committed to the saints. Orthodoxy then takes the place of righteousness; unction that calls itself "spiritual" takes the place of conscience; and the moral judgment may actually become so blunted as to tolerate in one's self conduct far beneath the standards of the world's people.

Such misplacements of emphasis make it expedient continually to recall our minds to some of the simplest, almost self-evident, principles of goodness, which are also principles of the spiritual life. For the time being let us forget all philosophical questions as to the relations of morals and religion, and even turn away from asking what is right and what is wrong, in order that we may concentrate attention upon some of the formal conditions of moral growth which are likewise conditions of spiritual vitality.

There are at least two qualities of character, which, being absent, render moral and
spiritual stability impossible, and being present, constitute the foundations of both the
moral and the spiritual building.   The first is
what may be called

## Downright Honesty.

In the most radical sense, honesty is the
purpose and the habit of seeing things, as far
as possible, just as they are.   It is the opposite of self-deception.   Self-deception is, if
possible, a more radical dishonesty than the
deception of others.   It is worse to be blind
than it is to raise a dust which temporarily
hides things from the eyes.   Whoever is dis-
honest with himself corrupts the faculties
through which alone he can guide himself to
any worthy end.

This truth led Socrates to utter that hard
saying of his, that to do wrong ignorantly is
worse than to do wrong knowingly.   He who
knowingly sins already sees the contrast between sin and righteousness; there is here
the possibility of going on from knowledge of
the right to decision in favor of it.   But he
whose faculties have ceased to give warning

lacks even this advantage. Now, insincerity with one's self is one of the processes, and one of the most fatal ones, whereby the normal entrances to the moral will are closed. He who forms a habit of not seeing things as they are, is like a pilot who should deliberately destroy his compass or put out his own eyes. Or, he is like a climber on a precipitous mountain who should destroy the trail in front of him.

There is no calamity, no unrighteousness, more dreadful than that of bringing our intellect into slavery to our desires. There is no more momentous aspect of our freedom than our ability to form a habit of regarding as true whatever we desire to have true. On the other hand, there is no more exalted function of the human will than that of maintaining judicial rectitude in the inmost thought.

The process of self-sophistication is a gradual one, and it takes many directions. One person indulges the thought of a desired thing that is wrong in some apparently slight degree; the thought of the thing increases the desire for it; as the desire grows, the scruple seems less worthy of attention. At last desire has its own way, and after the deed is done he questions whether it was wrong after all. From the query to a positive assertion that it was not wrong is a slight step. Then, assuming himself to be in the right, and taking his new level as a standard, he lets himself down by the same process to a still lower level. We may thus carry our standard down with us until we reach very low depths of moral degradation without clearly knowing it.

Another method of self-deception is more intellectual, since it consists in juggling with names so as to make a syllogism come out right. One of the severest tests of honesty is found in the naming of things intimately related to ourselves. How easy it is to call a thing by the name of some class of harmless objects with which it has some similarity, and then take the name as an adequate substitute for the thing. If we can only name something to suit ourselves, we can make logic itself defend us! We justify stinginess by saying that charity begins at home. We say that we commit errors or indiscretions, when the fact is, that we have sinned. We speak of speculating, when we ought frankly to say gambling. "Genius for business" paints avarice and oppression in rosy colors. A book-keeper or a bank clerk only carries the same thing a little further when he calls embezzlement "borrowing." How different would much of life look to us if the naming of things were not thus in the hands of interested parties!

There are still other ways of placing things under a desirable major premise. According to our changing exigencies, we shift the object from means to ends, and back from ends to means; from act to instrument, and back from instrument to act. The badness of a cause we transfer to the hearts of its defenders, and dislike of a person slides into disapproval of his acts, or depreciation of whatever is associated with his name. Zeal for a cause excuses cruelty to our opponents. The value of wealth as a means is transferred to wealth as an end. The sacredness of religion is extended to the instruments of religion, and finally to its representatives in our own persons, so that to disagree with us is to resist God.

The process of self-deception is of a kind to conceal even its own nature from us. We may degrade ourselves to almost any extent at the same time that we regard ourselves as good churchmen or even as saintly characters. We then become, to use a paradoxical term, unconscious hypocrites. The worst kind of hypocrite is not the one who tries to appear to others to be what he is not, but the one who deceives himself concerning himself. This is a vice before which both the victim and his friends stand helpless. He will employ no remedy because he cannot be convinced that he needs one. If you press one upon him, he will convince himself that you are a meddler or a persecutor of virtue. Strangely enough, some of these self-deceived persons, through the very completeness of the deception, make such an impression of sincerity as to become or to remain leaders of the people. The question is often a difficult one, whether this or that person who is doing great harm in the name of religion is conscious of insincerity or of imposture. It is not improbable that in most of these cases the standards of self-judgment have been so far destroyed as to make genuine self-knowledge practically impossible.

In view of this ability of ours to destroy our moral and spiritual insight at the same time that we believe it to be uncorrupted, would it not be a healthful exercise to remind ourselves now and then that a really good life must be built on reality? As all knowledge has some relation to the ends of human life, all self-deception must tend to evil. The severest, as it is the most fundamental, test of a good life might be put into these words, "Am I myself real?" Whoever sows unreality in the very faculties that distinguish reality from illusion is bound to reap failure and bitter disappointment, for only the real can abide.

On the other hand, any man who is downright honest with himself has some fellowship with spiritual things. There is hope for any man, however sunken he may be, who frankly recognizes his moral state. There is in him a germ of the good life. The reformation of the Prodigal Son began when "he came to himself." He had been not only living with swine, but what is worse, refusing to face the incongruity of it. He had persistently deceived himself into thinking that he was having a good time. The throwing off of the mask that hid him from himself was not only a preparation for the better life—it was the beginning of it. The man who is honest with himself has some ground for self-respect; he may on the same ground claim the respect of his fellows; we may even dare to say that God himself must respect him.

But we must not hide from ourselves the fact that every sinful act tends to destroy our capacity for truth. For sinning is itself an exchange of the real for the seeming. It is the taking of that which is not as though it were. No man can commit sin and be comfortable unless he enters upon this fatal road of self-sophistication. Desire first outweighs scruple; then it doubts the authority of the scruple; afterwards denies its authority; and thus, finally, inclination sits in the judge's chair. Hence, the honest man, if he is to retain his honesty, must also make a

*Determination to Do Right.*

This is a second foundation-stone of both the moral and the spiritual edifice. To talk about fidelity to duty is doubtless to raise a very trite subject, and yet, at the risk of triteness in our talk, we must strive not to let the thing itself grow trite. The tendencies thereto are many, and at some periods of history they are greater than at others. First, the inclination of the moment is always likely to blind us to the realities that are eternal, and self-indulgence always stands at our elbow to make the lesser or self-regarding good seem the greater. We have come into possession of human traits through a long series of slight advances upon an animal ancestry. The lower animals act almost altogether from impulse, and by so acting they attain their own highest good. Instinctive desire and impulse are enough to adjust them to their world, but our world is vastly greater than theirs, and adjustment to it calls for correspondingly greater mental powers. We have the animal instincts, and they perform their functions without needing stimulus from reason or conscience. But other functions essential to specifically human life cannot be left to instinct. They require rational consideration and conscious choice. Doubtless something of morality may be attained by a relatively thoughtless absorption of the ideas and usages of the moral persons in our environment, yet the highest morality requires moral thoughtfulness and a steady determination to do right.

Again, the idea of duty tends to be obscured by the extraordinary emphasis placed upon the notions of evolution and progress in our day. In popular thought, the idea of evolution has been hastily interpreted as though it smoothed out the differences between things, whereas it is founded upon the recognition of such differences, and exists for the sake of showing that relationships exist between things in spite of their differences. The existence of a law that relates unlike things in a single system has undoubtedly been taken to mean that at bottom there is no antithesis, but only all-alikeness. If at bottom all things are alike, moral distinctions are non-essential. If the essential thing in man is the animality from which he has evolved, then conscience is only an accretion. From this way of thinking it results, as I conceive, that the sharp edge of the "ought" and the "ought not" is being felt less than it ought to be for our moral health.

The difficulty is increased by a hazy conception of universal progress that associates itself with the notion of organic evolution. Many men appear to have drawn from evolution the inference that a self-executing law of the universe will take care of moral interests, so that the individual need not assume any special responsibility. This is an utter misunderstanding. What evolution teaches about moral interests is, that instinct prepares the way for reason, the latter being evolved just because there are interests which can be promoted only through self-conscious choice and individual effort. Evolution teaches in the most emphatic way that faculties exist to be used, and that only by the use of its latest and most highly developed faculties can any species conserve its own peculiar life, and prepare the way for a higher development of life. The very fact that we can deliberate, choose, feel a sense of responsibility is evidence that this is our proper function. The determination to do right is fundamental to human life in any full or distinctive sense.

A third factor that tends to obscure the significance of plain fidelity to duty is failure to perceive its spiritual or religious quality. We are still suffering from the mistake of those who, not many years ago, never tired of saying things derogatory to the merely moral man. One of the expressions by which men of that day uttered their contempt is, "the dirty rags of morality." Less than fifty years ago, a writer on "Natural Goodness" asserted that "moral men, as a class, and in virtue of their morality, inflict the severest injury on the cause of religion. . . . . The more perfect the moralist, the more fatal the influence.'' Dissenting from the notion that symmetrical morality has itself a religious character, the author declared that such morality "is purely a natural growth." The religious teachers of to-day have, of course, outgrown this standpoint, yet it may be doubted whether they have made clear that every genuine determination to do right has divine significance, and that fidelity to such a determination is fidelity to a spiritual principle of life. Surely God requires no more than that a man should be wholly devoted to duty. Even when we come to the privileges of religion, we are still within the sphere of duty, since whatever is worth while, that is, whatever is really good, carries with it an obligation to make effort for its attainment.

There is need of a clearing up of our notion of what constitutes a moral life. The fundamental fact of such a life is the recognition of a law that supersedes mere inclination. A moral man is one who habitually and of principle prefers to do his duty. He is faithful not merely to the duties that he likes to do, or to those that are convenient for him, for one who stops here is still under the dominion of inclination. Every horse-thief, pickpocket, seducer of innocence, does the duties he likes to do. The truly moral man, in a word, is one who surrenders his selfishness and self-will to a higher law.

This is not to say that one must be perfect in character and conduct before being entitled to the name of moral man. A man may fall from his moral purpose a thousand times without ceasing to be fundamentally moral, just as Christians do not cease to be Christians by falling into their besetting sins or failing to present a complete reproduction of the mind of Jesus. Neither morality nor religion consists in having attained any absolute standard, but rather in honest, self-surrendering aspiration toward a standard. The moral man is he who makes duty the central principle, the fundamental choice, of his life. He may do wrong, but he does not set out to do so, and he does not choose to continue in it. He may see things through imperfect eyes, and so he may regard as good many things that are bad. He is sure to be a man of like passions with other men, and so to have faults, many and sore. But none of these things reaches down to the fundamental choice by which alone can be determined what we call character.

Such a man denies himself, if need be, for conscience' sake. He will endure loss and hardship rather than let the one clear flame of a good conscience burn dim. He is honest toward religion. He welcomes truth, and intends to live according to it. His mind may have been confused through unfortunate early training, he may have honest doubts of what is commonly believed, but he is open to truth.

What shall be the attitude of religion toward a man like this? When Jesus looked upon a moral young man it is said that he loved him! What an awful thing would it be if, through our religious zeal, blind to the essential affinity between such a life and that of the highest religious devotion, we should cast slurs on it, and so repel it from the things that ought to be made attractive. May we have the wisdom to tell such men, as Jesus did, that they are not far from the kingdom of God!

Indeed, it appears that the rich young man's real defect was, that he was not wholly moral. He was self-satisfied and self-seeking to such a degree that when the test came he flinched. The duty that was hardest he would not do, and so he really wrought despite to the principles of a moral life. These principles, taken seriously, cannot be separated from the principles of a religious life. God himself is the supreme moral being, and surrender to duty is already, though sometimes unconsciously, surrender to his will. Any man who lives for the right has in him a germ of spiritual life, though he may not call it such, and though he may, through ignorance, miss many of the privileges of the sons of God. What he still needs is the revelation of God's loving fatherhood and of the ability of Jesus to fulfil—that is, to bring to its fulness—the law which he already acknowledges.

## The Message of Religion to the Merely Moral Man.

The practical outcome of our discussion at this point is twofold: it points to the duty of the church to take advantage of the spiritual leverage presented by the honest moral endeavors of men, and it suggests to moral men the possibility of carrying to a higher development the spiritual germ already within them.

Let the professedly moral man ask himself whether he is really moral, or whether he calls himself by that exalted name merely because he performs the duties that are not too distasteful to him. It is a very serious thing to take upon one's self such a title. Morality is no term to stand for the fact that society tolerates us, or that there are worse sins than those which we prefer to commit. The worst man in the world commits only the sins that he enjoys the fruits of. The message of religion is, "Be honest with yourself; do you make duty or self the supreme master of your life? Dare to call yourself by the right name. If what you have been calling a moral life consists in keeping up appearances while your private habits are unrighteous and unclean, or if it consists in merely limiting your inclinations instead of adopting a higher principle, then begin to-day to be whole-heartedly true to the noble name that you have claimed for yourself!"

Why do I call this the message of religion, whereas it is apparently only the message of morality? Because here religion and morality speak the same words. The two enter the heart and depart from it together, and the development of what is called morality is at the same time a development of spiritual capacities and functions. It is possible to worship God without naming him, and this is precisely what we do in every honest surrender of inclination to duty, in all devotion to the things that God loves. Accordingly, the message of religion to the merely moral man proceeds in this higher, prophetic tone: "Have I been so long with thee, and yet hast thou not known me? The higher law which thou callest duty, the voice within which thou callest conscience, this is thy spiritual nature. It is at once thy higher self and the Spirit of God. It is a point at which the Absolute Life so communicates himself to thy inmost soul that the highest human becomes indistinguishable from the divine. Thou art worshiping an unknown God, but it is thy privilege to find him declaring himself not only as law, but also as love. Listen to the instinctive voices of thy highest nature and thou shalt find that they are the voice of God. Following them thou shalt become consciously and joyously what in germ thou already art, a son of God!"

## *The Message of Morality to the Religious Man.*

The advice to be absolutely in earnest with matters of right and wrong is as appropriate for the professedly religious as it is for the professedly moral man.  For experience shows how easy it is to treat religion as something distinct from simple goodness.  Of course religion must not be reduced to mere obedience to a law.  It is vastly more than mere morality; it is the full corn in the ear, of which the recognition of duty is but the seed.  In religion our subjection to moral law transforms itself into a personal relationship of love and fellowship whence flow satisfactions for all sides of our higher nature.  Yet it is possible so to emphasize these additional elements of the complete man as to render religion one-sided.  An unethical religion is no better than an unreligious morality.  A religious experience that finds God in moments of special communion more than in moments of moral aspiration and endeavor involves not only danger of self-deception, but also a misrepresentation of Christ before the world.  We must warn ourselves against the old misconception of salvation, that assumes that if only we have faith we do not need to lay very much stress upon being good.

It is possible to treat religion as paupers treat the hands from which they beg, valuing it only for the personal satisfactions it brings. Like sons of wealth who grow up in idleness, those who allow themselves to share benefits without sharing responsibilities become flabby and unreliable. Reposing in the thought of God's free salvation, one may forget to be a worker together with God. Glorying in the cross of Christ, we easily forget that if we are to share in his glory, we must also be partners with him in his sufferings.

It is almost a pity that we cannot be persecuted for righteousness' sake, for persecution develops vigor. The perils to spirituality in a time when there are few visible obstacles to a religious life are greater than at any other time. The hermit-crab, which takes possession of the shell of another marine animal, never venturing beyond its safe shelter, becomes soft and pulpy in all parts except the members that are actively employed in reaching outward into the external world. So, when we allow ourselves to settle down in the

*why worry? Be righteous — you will be persecuted*

temple of the Lord with little or no sense of responsibility, we lose the firmness of fiber, the power of resistance, the habit of aggressiveness, that constitutes one essential part of a normal religious life.

Not a few religious teachers appear to be afraid lest the increasing emphasis that is being placed upon the ethical aspects of religion may lead us to neglect its other elements. But fears of this sort are based upon the outworn assumption that moral qualities are not also spiritual qualities. When our devotion to the moral becomes pure and complete, we find morality itself leading toward that rounding out of the higher nature which finds only its beginning in obedience to impersonal duty. What we need is not less stress upon the ethical, but a more thorough development of it. There is no danger that this generation will feel the sternness of the "ought" and "ought not" too keenly, but there is danger that it will not realize that duty is the

"Daughter of the Voice of God."

# THE CHIEF END OF MAN

# CHAPTER VI

## THE CHIEF END OF MAN

According to a Greek myth, the Theban sphinx was accustomed to propound to men a single question. Whosoever first solved it was to gain irresistible power over the questioner, but whoever failed to give the correct answer forfeited his life. The question was, "What animal goes on four legs in the morning, on two at noon, and on three at night?" Œdipus guessed the riddle by answering that this animal is man, who in infancy crawls, at maturity walks, and in old age employs a walking stick to assist his legs. Under this pictorial form Greek thought expressed its sense of the mystery of human existence. Whoso solves this problem becomes master of all things, but whoso fails to solve it forfeits all.

One great motive power of religious and philosophical thought has always been the desire to understand ourselves and our place in the universe. A Hebrew poet-thinker, considering the heavens, the work of God's

fingers, the moon and the stars which he has or-
dained, speedily discovers that interest in creation centers in humanity—"What is man?"
In a curiously similar spirit, Plato breaks into
poetry, and the resulting lines are the only
specimen of his verse that has come down to
us. They have been rendered as follows:

> "Thou gazest at the stars, my Life;
>   Would I might be
>   Yon starry skies
>   With thousand eyes,
>   That I might gaze on thee!"

It was the same interest that led the West-
minster divines to give the first place in their
catechism to the question, "What is the chief
end of man?" The answer, "The chief end
of man is to glorify God, and to enjoy him
forever," stood for generations as the accepted interpretation of the Christian view of
life.

## Self-Regarding Other-Worldliness.

The meaning that used to be found in
these words of the catechism is clearly explained by the comments of Thomas Watson,
a British divine of the days of Cromwell.
Glorifying God, according to him, consists in

four things: appreciation, adoration, affection, and subjection. "This," he adds, "is the yearly rent we pay to the crown of heaven." The meaning of life, according to this, is to be found in a sort of bargain according to which God leases to men certain privileges in order that he may reap certain advantages for himself, and men pay the rental because of advantages to be gained thereby. The Creator likes to be praised and worshiped; men want to go to heaven; an exchange is effected whereby each secures what he desires.

Note two implications of this exposition. First, it assumes that both God and men are actuated by self-regarding motives. It simply ignores the possibility of disinterestedness. God creates man, and man worships God, "for revenue only." To the question, "Why should I tell the truth, or be kind to the unfortunate?" the reply was simple: "Because, if you do these things, you will go to heaven; if you do them not, you will be punished in hell." The whole scheme is parallel with the method employed by some parents to secure good conduct from their children. Do so or so, and I will give you a sugar-plum, etc. Of course the theory leaked, and the practice was better than the theory. The love of God for men could not be twisted into a selfish affection, nor sympathy on our part toward our fellows be reduced to the terms of a bargain. Nevertheless, it remained for very recent times to make clear to the general consciousness that the divine motive and the Christian motive are just the opposite of self-seeking.

A second implication of this view is that it postpones the realization of our true life to the future world. At present, it teaches, we are not exactly living, but rather preparing to live. Life on earth is simply a probationary process whereby the good and the bad are being sorted out from each other in order that each may enter upon an appropriate mode of existence after death. The most soul-searching question that preachers of this earlier day knew how to ask was, ''Are you prepared to die?''

Devout sentiment, as a consequence, took the form of ''other-worldliness.'' Hymnology became saturated with it. The last stanza of hymns commonly contained some reference to death and the future life. Men and women actually sang their contempt for the life that now is. They declared that they were pilgrims and strangers in a foreign land through which they were passing because it was the only route to their home. Even little children were taught to sing, "I want to be an angel."

When little Harriet Beecher presented herself to a Hartford clergyman to be examined as to her fitness to join the church, this heart-searching question, among others, was propounded: "Harriet, do you feel that if the universe should be destroyed [awful pause] you could be happy with God alone?" The biographer says: "After struggling in vain, in her mental bewilderment, to fix in her mind some definite conception of the meaning of the sounds which fell on her ear like the measured strokes of a bell, the child of fourteen stammered out, "Yes, sir.""

Let us not be too severe toward this honest attempt to interpret the great mystery of human life. It is not easy, at any time, to say what is the fundamental need and what the supreme aim of human life. The other-worldly attitude toward life, in spite of its gruesome narrowness of vision, did at least emphasize the truth that there is a higher law for life than self-will and unregulated impulse; that the real world goes deeper than things of sense; that this temporal life is related to eternity; and that God is the central verity of all.

Then, as now, of course, life had its own way of breaking through the fences of inadequate observation and mistaken reasoning. Souls that were sensitive to beauty could not help feeling that earth is more than their religion gave it credit for being. Men and women who had experienced the joys of human affection, and the blessedness of serving others, knew that this life is more than a waiting-room, more than a probation; that it is even life itself, an end and not merely a means to something else, and that it may be full of its own reward. Finally, under the spell of the life of Jesus men could not help finding the heart of God, and actual religion became something very different from a bargain.

These influences and others have necessitated a reinterpretation of the Christian view of life. This reinterpretation centers around the idea or obligation of

*Seeking First the Kingdom of God.*

When Jesus spoke on the great problem of the meaning of life—the problem of philosopher, poet, and prophet—he said three things of first-class significance: First, be not anxious for your physical life, but seek first the kingdom and righteousness of God, and all needful *things* will be added to you; second, do not try to save your life (or soul), for if you do you will lose it, whereas, only as you lose your life (or soul) can you save it; finally, the great commandments are that we love God with all our powers, and our neighbor as ourself.

These pronouncements used, it is true, to be adduced in support of the view that has just been condemned, but by utterly mistaken methods of reading the Bible. For example, Jesus' most characteristic term, the kingdom of God, which he used interchangeably with the kingdom of heaven, was incorrectly identified with heaven, the state or place of the glorified dead. John the Baptist and Jesus both began their preaching by announcing the kingdom of heaven as at hand—not far off in time or in space, not something to be waited for, but something right here and now. In exact harmony with this we are taught to pray that this kingdom may come upon earth by the doing of God's will here as it is done in heaven. With this agree the parables of the sower, the tares, the mustard-seed, the leaven, and the dragnet. One who showed appreciation of the law of love was declared to be not far from the kingdom. When Jesus was asked when the kingdom of God should come, he replied that it is not something to be watched for or looked forward toward, with a "Lo, here," or a "Lo, there," when it comes, but rather something already among us.

The probably mistaken reading of this passage, as though it declared the kingdom to be within us, a matter of heart or disposition rather than something external and visible, serves to draw attention to another misinterpretation of Jesus' teaching that has been employed in support of the other-worldly view of life. The passage in question is most naturally interpreted as meaning that the kingdom of heaven is "among you" or "in your midst." The contrast is not that between an external and an internal kingdom, but between a kingdom to be looked for in the future and one that is already set up among us. When it became necessary to admit that the kingdom of God is not identical with future blessedness, other-worldliness seized

upon the translation "within you," to show
that the kingdom that now is, is simply a disposition of the heart.   If the heart be right,
we have been taught, all will be well.   But this
is really little more than a reflection of the old
notion that the business of life is getting ready
for heaven.   The reasoning was something
like this: Since it is the pure in heart that
shall see God, get your heart right now, and
to that extent the kingdom of heaven is already
within you.

But, while the kingdom of God is a matter
of the heart, it is no more truly an inner principle than an outer organization of life.   It is
not to remain hidden within the depths of the
meal, but to fill and give life to the whole.
The entire environment is to be transformed
so as to participate in it.   After reading the
Sermon on the Mount, who can imagine that
Christianity is any more a religion of the heart
than of outward and visible act?   It is solely
by their fruits that we are to discern men's
relation to the Christ.   The climax of the
whole discourse is the parable about the doers
of the word.

The whole philosophy of Christianity centers about the idea of bringing the divine or

spiritual out of the invisible by incarnating it in the visible. Incarnation is vastly more than an event that occurred two thousand years ago; it is the central principle, or shall we say fact, of every Christian life. The divine life is to dwell within our life in such a way as to become visible, a light set upon a hill. It is an outward-going impulse; or rather, it is both impulse and act, both an internal disposition and a visible organization of life.

The Christian conception of life is all contained in that of the kingdom of God. This kingdom is at once an internal, organizing principle and the resulting external organization. This organization embraces the life that now is and that which is to come. Its motive-power is love to God and to men, and this is not an individualistic but a social motive. The older conception of the Christian life was ruled by the notion of securing personal salvation. The motive was assumed to be self-regarding. If the term salvation is slipping out of use, the chief reason is probably the fact that a better understanding of the mind of Christ has made it impossible for us to accept the selfish motive which that term implied.

In this substitution of a social for an
vidual end is found the clew to the remark
paradox about saving and losing life.
who seeks to save his soul, that is, he who
life proceeds from self-regarding motives, lose
his soul.  He cannot even be himself.  But
he who, like Jesus, takes as his own and only
good the good of the whole society of which
he is a part, though he gives up his soul,
nevertheless finds it.

This is an astonishing pronouncement.
Would Jesus tell us that the only thing that I
can enjoy, my own happiness, I must not seek
after?  Is it not visionary folly thus to condemn our natural and inevitable desire for
self-satisfaction?  Let us not misunderstand
Jesus' words, or hastily assume that they run
counter to human experience.  Jesus does
not condemn desire for our own happiness;
he merely enables us to see it in perspective.
I am, indeed, to love my neighbor as myself,
but this means that I am to love myself as
my neighbor.  I am to be *an* end, but not
*the* end, of my own conduct.  I am to count
as one and only one, and even so only in connection with the organic whole to which I
belong.  Apart from it, I cannot count as

even one. There is no purely private good. In short, I am to measure all things from the standpoint of a social whole, of which I am simply one of many members. When a hand gathers food, it does so for the whole body, itself included, and apart from the general nutrition of the body, there could be no nutriment for the hand. In a parallel way, Jesus would have the whole of our self-chosen activities directed to the social good; and he declares that if we try to live a life other than that of the social body, we shall lose our very selves, we shall be dehumanized, and miss the satisfactions which we seek.

Christian self-denial must be understood as an application of this principle. It is easily misunderstood. The Buddha taught a self-denial that has often been compared with that inculcated by Jesus, but the two are opposed in principle, though in many circumstances they lead to similar acts. Buddhism advises us to forget self in the service of others, it is true, but the end in view is a personal redemption from the pains of existence. Self-denial, in this scheme, becomes simply an exchange of lesser satisfactions for the sake of attaining the Buddhist heaven. The motive is not socialized.

Christian asceticism made a similar mistake. Some ascetics apparently believed that the suppression of self, the negation of the human, is *per se* pleasing to God, and brings its reward in heaven. The practices based upon this view are obviously un-Christian because their basal motive is unsocial. Perhaps a larger part of ascetic practices rested upon the notion of the superior sanctity of a life of religious contemplation, and of the help that self-suppression gives to contemplation. By crucifixion of the body, and even of the mind, mystical communion with God was supposed to be attained—a communion filled with the joys of heaven. Here, again, the motive is unsocial, and therefore un-Christian. Though the ascetic preach the gospel to sinners, though he relieve human suffering, though he give his body to be burned, and have not the social motive, it profiteth him nothing.

Christian self-denial has a positive, not a negative, aim, and this positive aim is social. We deny self, in the Christian sense, when we make the interest of others our own interest. And this, let it be noted, is the very opposite of self-suppression, for in thus losing our life we save it. Christianity is not self-suppression, but self-realization. Its advice is to be completely human, to be completely ourselves, but to remember that this is possible only through participation in the life of our fellows. The end of the individual life is a perfected community life. This, once more, is not to be worked for as a means to my individual self-realization, for this would place my interest above that of the community, whereas I must reach the point of consciously identifying my personal good with the common good.

## Is the Kingdom of God a Visionary Scheme?

Is Jesus' interpretation of life a mere dream, or is it rather the wisdom of God and the power of God? How shall we answer this question? There is only one way, and that is to examine life as we have found it. Every one of us knows something of what it is really to live. Every one has experienced at times, in greater or less degree, the something of realization that enables one to say, "Now

I am myself; this, in some degree, is the attainment of true life."

It is the open secret of the world that such self-realization does not come through self-seeking or self-centered enjoyment. We do not need to go to the Scriptures to find out that no man liveth to himself and no man dyeth to himself. Even before the human species is reached in the evolutionary order, the quasi-social solidarity of many species prophesies the true significance of the individual. Specifically human life is possible only through regard of one for another: of mother for child, of the members of the family for one another, of the individual for his clan, his tribe, his people, his race. To-day there is a general confession that Aristotle was right when he pronounced man a social animal, and declared an individual existence apart from society to be something less than human.

The truth of this principle lies open before every eye. Family affection, through which one realizes one's life by mingling its hopes and joys, its labors and sorrows, with those of another, is a standing witness to the truth that self-realization comes only through the sharing of a social good. Why is love between the sexes so interesting to the whole world? What has made it the *motif* of such a vast proportion of our literature, our music, our dramatic art? A biologist will naturally and properly answer that the instinct of sex is one of the two most important to life, the instinct for food being the other. But why does the one so completely overshadow the other as an intellectual and artistic interest? Why, unless the social element present in one and lacking in the other is a superior and more characteristic concern of humanity? Food-seeking is primarily individualistic, and therefore prosy; love carries the individual beyond himself, and is therefore poetic.

It is remarkable, also, how completely the artistic interest and the moral interest intertwine. Love, as self-realization through devotion to another, meets our moral approbation, and awakens æsthetic pleasure. But when the instinct of sex is corrupted to purely selfish uses, our whole nature cries out against it. Thus corrupted in motive, it becomes the cause of the evil which, more than anything else, deserves to be called the despair of society. It buys and sells that which is beyond price, and under the false guise of self-realization, withers the very capacities of the soul on which self-realization depends.   Because it seeks life where life cannot be found, it produces a festering sore of body and of soul, and whelps all manner of crime and destruction.   On the other hand, marriage entered upon and lived through as a mutual interest, as a community life in which each makes the good of the other his own equal good, has been and is a bulwark of all that men reckon worth while in life.   Love seeks to give rather than to get.   All the world loves a lover, not for his self-seeking, but for his devotion to the object of his love.   The world's experience stamps as truly human such love as this.

He who has never been carried out of his particular self-consciousness by a noble enthusiasm for some common good knows not what it is to live.   Even childhood friendships and immature affections among boys and girls are not altogether insignificant, for they do at least foreshadow the meaning of life, and in many cases, doubtless, they give direction to life's motives.   The enthusiasm of a college student for his class, his fraternity, or his athletic team, whatever temptations it may bring, is an expression of the higher, not of the lower, nature. Loyalty to church, enthusiasm for a cause, pride in one's city or one's state, love of one's country—all these are signs of life, especially when they do not end in vociferation, but go on to active service. Yes, the service of our fellows is real life. Even to die on the battle-field in the cause of freedom is life. To risk, to give, to labor, to suffer for others is life. One is human, one is one's self only when one can say, "I live, yet not I, but my family, my church, my country, humanity lives in me!" Jesus was not a visionary.

The love of men is an organizing principle, while self-seeking tends to disorganization. This is clearly true of the family, but men do not always perceive that the principle applies also to all the collective activities of men. We are at last beginning to see, however, that it applies to civil states. Government is not the organized selfishness of the citizens of a state, but just the reverse. Mere self-seeking in an official or in a voter tends to the corruption and the dissolution of government, while safety and perpetuity depend upon the social

sense which we call patriotism.    Men associate themselves into states, as into families,
then, because something larger than the individual lives and speaks within each of them.
Some day we shall acknowledge that precisely
the same law holds for the relations between
nations and for the industrial and commercial
organization.

Glimmerings of such insight are plentiful
already.    Wars of aggression are discredited
by the conscience of the Western World, and
men are prophesying a day when, driven
thereto by the fact of a world-wide commercial
solidarity, if by nothing more sentimental,
standing armies will be reduced or disbanded,
and international disputes will be settled by
peaceful means.    Again, competition, as the
basic principle of men's business relations to
one another, has refuted its own claims by its
effects in practice.    For, when competition
had conceived and brought forth, the offspring
was found to be, not individualism, but combination.    The corporations and the labor
unions of our day give their testimony, as
does the family life, to the truth of Jesus'
teaching, that the real interests of life are
mutual.

Possibly competition in some form will always be needful as a means of bringing the individual to his greatest efficiency, but it must be an expression of a social need, not of unsocial individualism. There is a competition that is substantially a war of each against all. It must pass away, because it is based upon a mistaken conception of reality. Individualism defeats itself because men are not and cannot be mere individuals, cannot save their life by any possible self-seeking.

Doubtless the great combinations of capital and of labor are due in large degree to self-regarding motives. But to precisely that extent they are and must be in unstable equilibrium. Sooner or later they must surrender their own individualism in order to become instruments of the social good. In fact, through a mixture of not clearly defined motives, the captains of industry are causing to be forged mighty tools for doing the world's work. It is as if some invisible, titanic power were working within these men, and making them the unconscious agents of a great purpose. The ultimate forms of industrial and political organization toward which we are moving we may not as yet clearly discern, but of one thing we may have a reasonable assurance: Since the growing tendency to organization rests upon an actual mutuality of interests, its results must ultimately become a means for bringing this mutuality to men's consciousness, and so for making the community interest more and more the controlling motive in men's dealings the one with another. Warfare between capital and labor will cease, not by the conquest of one over the other, but by the submission of both to the whole, of which they are only parts. Employer and employee will some day recognize the plain fact that neither of them is here to be ministered unto, but to minister. Both will go to their daily occupation in the peace and the joy of those who serve their fellowmen. Seeking first this social righteousness, each will find his proper share of things added unto him. The factory owner and the factory operative alike will feel, what is the plainest truth, that the original and fundamental reason for the existence of any manufacturing establishment is that its products minister to humanity. The true value of an invention or of improved methods of manufacture is determined solely by their ability to promote the ends of civilization. In short, just because of the eternal truth of Jesus' paradox about saving and losing life, industrial progress cannot help ministering, in one way or another, to the realization of social ideals. The kingdoms of this world, civil and industrial, must become the kingdoms of our Lord and of his Christ.

In all departments of human life it is the intention of Jesus that his kingdom should become an external and visible fact as well as an internal and invisible disposition of the heart. In the church the divine is incarnated. Wherever followers of the Christ live in communion with one another, there is the visible kingdom of God. This part of the kingdom, as well as other parts, is a growing, uncompleted life. The union of the disciples is only gradually achieved. But the inner principle of all the churches has in it a life that is bursting the bands of exclusiveness, and bringing in a higher and higher unity. The vital principle of all the churches will ultimately require of all of them that they surrender their own individualism in order to found a world-wide, visible fellowship. The union that Jesus had in mind when he prayed that his followers might all be one is a visible union, for it is to

be to the world a manifestation of Christ.
Just as God was sensibly revealed in Christ,
so Christ is to become visible to the world
through the union of Christians. Such a
union is bound to come through the very
nature of the life principle involved in Christian discipleship.

The kingdom becomes visible not only in the
church, but also wherever men put Christian
principles into practice in the relations of man
to man. Wherever a man and a woman
found a family upon genuine love, it is their
privilege to say that there, in the home and in
all the occupations and appointments that
minister to its maintenance, is the kingdom of
God. So it is with every philanthropy and
with all the institutions of education and of art
that minister to the real life of men. Not less
is it true of every business and profession that
supplies any actual need or in any way pro-
motes the ends of civilization. Civil government, too, though for indefinite ages to come
it may maintain its separation from the church,
can have no legitimate purposes other than
those of the kingdom. Even now democracy's proclamation that government exists
for the good of the governed goes a long way

toward identifying its functions with those of the kingdom of God. Whatever, in fact, helps toward the realization of a perfected society belongs to the kingdom. Jesus must reign until he has put all things under his feet. He proposes that his own spirit of love take possession of every instrument and institution in order that they may fill to the full their mission of social good.

Men fancy, of course, that in their daily occupations they are merely looking out for number one. But they are building wiser than they know. There is within them a human heart that is essentially, and not incidentally, social, and out of this heart are the issues of life. Men cannot escape this, which is their very selves. Without deliberate intention, their labor, for the most part, does now fulfil a social mission. The laboring man, the artisan, the capitalist, the professional man, all contribute to the common stock of good that goes under the name of civilization. Some day they must become clearly conscious of this, their larger, more inspiring calling. They will reckon self-seeking as loss, and will count their profits in terms of the social good. Will they then

have less for themselves?   Some will doubtless have more things and some will have
fewer, but all will be wealthier because all
will live more.   Losing the life of selfish
gaining and selfish spending, they will find
life all the more full of self-realization.

The kingdom of God is not a visionary
scheme.   It defines for us what has always
constituted the most real and the most rich
factor of life.   It formulates a principle that
lies imbedded in the whole of those relations—
domestic, social, industrial, and civil—that
constitute what is called civilization.   It is
the real goal of whatever of humanity there is
in us men.   It is the reality of our life, and
all that contradicts it has only illusory existence.   There is no genuine success in life, or
motive for life, or prospect of good for the
race, that is not rooted in it.

## What is it to Glorify God and to Enjoy Him Forever?

Returning to our starting-point, let us ask
ourselves what is the chief end of man.   Is it
to glorify God?   Yes; but glorifying God consists in uniting ourselves with him in heart
and work, to produce an ideal human race.

Loving God with all our powers means that we make his interest and his good our own.

Make God's good our own? Dare we include God himself in the social whole which it is our mission to live for? We may well be modest when we try to think God's thought concerning himself, and yet we but apply Jesus' own teachings when we say that the love of God toward men, and his desire for love in return, indicate some sort of solidarity of life. Here let us reverently pause, pushing back the speculative questions that press upon us, threatening to fill with curiosity a mind that needs inspiration. Let us hold fast to the thought that individualism no more expresses the life of God than it describes the real life of men. God, as well as man, is a social being. Glorifying him, accordingly, is no interplay between two mere individuals, each of whom seeks his own particular ends, but rather the maintenance of such an intimate relationship between the human and the divine existence as enables each to realize his life in the life of the other.

Is it our end to enjoy God forever? Yes, but not as compensation for our obedience to him. It is a sign of moral health that men have so largely ceased to be interested in the question of rewards and punishments. We are not to be good in order to gain bliss or to escape misery. The future life is not a device for getting even with men, or for reinforcing the motives to goodness, or for patching up a universe that is rather badly put together. Nor is this life a mere vestibule to real living. Rather, this life and the future life are one life. The logic of immortality is to be sought in that of the mutuality of the human and the divine. God lives in us, and we live in God; the eternal abides in the temporal, and the temporal in the eternal. To think of either apart from the other is to make an abstraction; to act as though they could be separated is the essence of badness and impiety. That the good man should enjoy God forever means that God as well as man is a social being, and that he is in earnest when he enters into social relations with us his creatures. These relations go to the center of his being, as they go to the center of ours. When God gives us himself, time, with its modification called death, ceases to be significant. The eternal is already ours, and heaven belongs to us. The heaven that

is to be is identical with the kingdom that now
is, a community of finite souls progressively
realizing their union with one another and with
the eternal life of God.

# THE RIGHT TO BE CALLED A
## CHILD OF GOD

# CHAPTER VII

## THE RIGHT TO BE CALLED A CHILD OF GOD

What is it to be a Christian? This question must be answered by appealing directly to Jesus. To-day, more than for many centuries, Christian thought realizes that he is the one full and complete source of Christianity properly so called. Would you know what God is? Behold him revealed in Jesus. Would you know what man is? Again, behold him revealed in Jesus. Would you know what a man must do in order to become a child of God? Note those whom Jesus received as his followers, and what demands he made upon those whom he sought for disciples. He is a Christian, in any age of the world, who fulfils the conditions of discipleship which Jesus exacted.

### The Simplicity of the Gospel.

The question that we propose to ourselves leaves entirely out of consideration what goes on in the mind of God with reference to those who turn from sin to righteousness. The simple message of the Gospel is that God loves us and is willing to accept us as children if only we are willing to be children. Immeasurable confusion has been wrought in thoughtful and conscientious souls by the custom of setting side by side, as though they were equally significant, the demands which Jesus makes upon us on the one hand, and on the other hand, the church's official view of how God can be reconciled to a sinner, and what he works in the secret recesses of the repentant sinner's heart. Instead of defining discipleship by the conditions which we must fulfil on our part, it has been defined and described by God's attitudes and acts, or even by some product of a supposed psychology of the divine being. Would-be Christians have had their attention fixed more upon expected or desired signs of what is going on in the divine consciousness than upon their own plain duty and privilege.

Looked upon thus as a transaction in a transcendental world, the entrance upon conscious discipleship has been too largely given over to theorists and mystics. It was only an extreme case of a widespread fact when some misguided pastors tested "seekers" by putting the question, "Are you willing to accept the plan of salvation?"  The other side of the error was contained in the instruction which led one thus willing to be saved to search his consciousness for signs and wonders from on high.  "It is essential to a distinct Christian consciousness," says a defender of these methods, "that the believer shall receive some preternatural manifestation that does not come under the laws of ordinary mental movement." This "divine revealment is not a mental process, though the mind conveys, according to its ability, what the spirit reveals."  How far is all this from the plain, practical preaching of Jesus!  It would be well for the churches that have fallen into such errors in the method of presenting the Gospel to ask themselves whether they have not brought upon themselves the indifference with which the masses regard evangelistic efforts.

A plain, business-like attitude toward religion more nearly resembles the attitude of Jesus than does that of the mere theologian or of the mere mystic.  It is conceded that Mark's non-mystical picture of the Master is nearer the facts in point of time and contains less subjective coloring than that of John. The latter was a mystic theologian, who confessedly wrote his version of the Gospel history in order to establish a doctrinal point of view. Unquestionably the teachings of Jesus, and Jesus himself as a historical phenomenon, furnish legitimate impulse and inexhaustible material for theoretic thought. Similarly, Christian experience has a vast range of possibilities. But Jesus' teachings are so profound, and his personality is so great, that their practical application is simple. It is so with all the great forces and laws of the universe. In spite of their vast range and complexity, practical adjustment for the essential purposes of life is always simple. A child of a year can adjust its body to the fact of gravitation so as to walk, though the law of universal attraction be sufficient to tax the highest human intelligence in the attempt to think it in its essence and its relations. The expansive power of steam can be utilized by an ordinary mechanic, though the theory of gases is far beyond his mental reach. To be or become a Christian is undoubtedly to illustrate truths of unmeasured breadth and of unsounded depth, yet the practical principles of Christianity are as simple as learning to walk.

In view of our previous discussion of the kingdom of God, we can go at once to the heart of the question. Jesus' great practical concern was the kingdom of God, that men should enter it and devote themselves to furthering it. Whoever takes sides with Christ in this, his supreme interest and concern, is a Christian. The essential requirement is that we choose this side and proceed to work for it. Any one can be a follower of Jesus and a child of God who desires the success of the kingdom of God strongly enough to throw his life into its common life.

What could be simpler? Suppose some one should come to you with the question, "What is it to be a Republican?" You would answer that a Republican is one who votes the Republican ticket. If the inquirer should then ask how he himself can become a member of this party, you would again reply, "By voting the Republican ticket." If, finally, he should demand to know how he may be sure that he is a genuine Republican, you would once again answer that voting this ticket and a fixed intention to vote it are all that is necessary. One becomes a Republican, remains a Republican, and establishes his status as a Republican simply by voting that way. Just so, one becomes a Christian by putting one's self on that side, continues a Christian by active loyalty to Christian ideals, and if one has no other way of knowing that one is a Christian and a child of God, the decision to be one and the voluntary devotion of one's powers to the ends of the kingdom constitute adequate evidence. Even the mystic John recognizes the validity of this test when he says that we may know that we have passed from death to life through the fact of our active love to our brethren.

This, in a nutshell, answers the question "What is it to be a Christian?" It neither denies nor affirms any of the traditional propositions concerning God's part in the transaction of becoming a child of God, nor does it propose that any single intellectual or emotional formula be gone through by all who wish to come to Christ. It seeks only to reduce to its lowest terms the vital conditions which we must meet if we would be disciples, and this it does by direct application to the individual life of Jesus' teachings concerning the kingdom of God.

What remains is to remove several misunderstandings that have been kept alive by an entirely natural misinterpretation of several passages of Scripture, particularly those employing the terms repentance, conversion, faith, love, and the new birth.

## The Volitional Element in Repentance and Conversion.

When Jesus came into Galilee preaching, and saying "Repent!" he added, "for the kingdom of heaven is at hand." The repentance that leads to discipleship, then, is in essential relation to the idea of the kingdom. What this relation is becomes clear from the Greek term here employed. Two New Testament words have been translated by the same English word, repent, but the two do not mean the same. They are brought together and contrasted in 2 Corinthians, vii. 10. Here "repentance to salvation" employs the word used in the Galilean preaching, while "not to be repented of" translates a very different term, and one that embodies a very different idea. The former signifies a change of mental attitude, such as we describe by saying that a man has "gone over" to another party; the latter designates the state of regretfulness, or sorrow. One is an attitude of mind involving a decision; the other is an emotion. The repentance of the Galilean preaching is something that we do; the other kind is something that we feel. We might freely paraphrase Jesus' command to repent as follows: "Your attitude toward life, your point of view, your standard of values is defective. You are living for self, and even estimating God's goodness by merely personal and national benefits. You have not known the wideness of the heart of God or of the heart of man. I announce to you the kingdom of God, the reign of universal love, and command that you reverse the principle of your life in accordance therewith." Whoever makes this change from self to the kingdom of God, weighing life in these new scales, repents in the Christian sense of that term.

A corresponding volitional element is fundamental in the term conversion, also. It is likewise significant that Jesus connected conversion, as well as repentance, directly with the notion of the kingdom of God. In every way conversion, as used in the New Testament, stands in the closest relation to repentance. The latter, literally translated, means a change of mind, while conversion, similarly translated, means a thorough turning. Repentance has to do with our standard of values. It consists in throwing away a false measure and accepting a true one. Conversion, in the New Testament sense, consists in making practical and controlling in life the results of this reweighing of issues.

By an entirely natural process, this original, very simple use of the word has been broadened, at least in popular speech, so as to make conversion cover practically everything supposed to be associated with the fact originally designated by it. Permit a homely illustration of this mode of extending the use of terms. The other day I received notice of an approaching banquet. Inscribed in one corner were the words, "Two dollars a plate." Here a single instrument employed at a banquet is used to designate a whole series of facts more or less distantly associated with it. So it is with conversion. A word originally descriptive of a simple process of volition has come to stand for I know not how many other things in our consciousness, and even in the divine mind.

When the Prodigal Son "came to himself,"
he threw away his old, false estimates of life,
and adopted new and sound ones. This was
repentance. Then came conversion, expressed
in the "I will arise," and realized in the act
of arising. The two are so closely connected
that either term might well cover the whole
process. Conversion is the act of the sinner
himself. No one can doubt this who reads
the New Testament in the Greek. Whoever
turns away from a life of sin to a life of obedience to Christian principle is a converted
man. Saying this does not deny, but merely
leaves out of consideration the part that God
plays in co-operation with the repentant sinner. It challenges nothing that you can believe on that point. It grants full liberty to
believe that only by empowering from on high
can one repent or be converted, and that the
preference for higher things manifested by a
converted man is begotten in him by an infusion of life from above. It merely insists
upon the plain fact that, according to the New
Testament, to be converted is to adopt the
Christian principle of life, that this is an act
of the sinner's own will, and that his status in

the kingdom can therefore be determined by what he chooses to be and to do.

Because repentance and conversion are thus our acts, they can be commanded, and thus the gospel comes to us not only with good news, but also with a "thou shalt."   If it be asked how one can be commanded to estimate the goods or apparent goods of life by any particular standard, the answer may again recite the story of the Prodigal Son, "When he came to himself."   The standards of value commanded by Christ are not foreign to our nature or merely imposed upon us.   It would be senseless to command me to regard as of supreme value, or even as valuable at all, anything that has no essential correspondence with the actual needs of my constitution. If you urge me to like caviar, I will reply that liking this delicacy must be left to the caprice of individual taste.   But tell me that I ought to weigh my acts by their probable effect upon my future as well as by the immediate satisfaction that they yield, and I can make no demurrer, because you have given voice to my own self.   Now, the Gospel must stand or fall by a similar ability to interpret us to ourselves. When it commands us to lay aside one set of estimates and adopt a different one, it will succeed, in the long run, if it is working with and not against what is deepest in us (whether what is deepest is merely "natural," or whether it is "through grace"), but it will fail if it lacks this fundamental adaptation. The command to repent, then, is a summons to let our inmost self, our real self, pass upon the motives and the ideals of life. The authority of such a command is exactly parallel with that of reason itself when it commands us to think in accord with the canons of self-consistency.

This brings us to the parallel question as to

### How Faith and Love can be Commanded.

As in the matter of repentance and conversion, so here the sensibleness of the command rests upon the volitional element in Christian faith and in Christian love.

The confusion of Christian faith with intellectual belief, which is simply a probable judgment, has wrought much havoc. Many have failed to see the absurdity of commanding one to hold for true what one sees no reason for so holding, or the futility of forbidding one to hold as probably true what seems to have a preponderance of evidence in its favor. To see the preponderance of evidence is to believe, while consciousness of failure to find reasons for or against is tantamount to consciousness of inability to have an opinion. My holdings-for-true cannot be commanded by another or by myself. The most that can be done is to present the appropriate evidence and then urge me to be wholly faithful to myself in the use of my intellectual powers. It may well be that when I thus employ my mind impartially upon a given set of facts and considerations, I shall reach a certain conviction, but this conviction must rest upon its own inner laws, not being imposed upon me, but developed from within in accordance with the essential laws of intelligence.

It is sometimes assumed that in the Christian life something other than evidence enables us to decide what is or is not true. If this were so, the inquisition might be able to prove its Christian character. For, if I can rightfully choose what I will hold for true, then I may incur any degree of guilt through my mere opinions. But it is time to have done with this whole dreary misunderstanding. Jesus had too much common sense to dream of proposing anything so dishonorable, not to say impossible. Christian faith is something that can be commanded without nonsense. Like repentance, it has its roots in the will, though both repentance and faith are closely connected with the functions of intellect.

Faith, then, is not a special process whereby we produce intellectual conviction without employing intellectual standards; it is not a method of cognition at all, nor does it consist in holding anything to be true. In respect to certainty and uncertainty, its function is the practical adjustment of life where evidence alone is an inadequate guide. Suppose that the future life were so purely hypothetical as not to be able, by any rational considerations pro or con, to become a determining factor in conduct. Suppose, nevertheless, that the unknown fact, whatever it is, is of real importance to us here and now, so that conduct according to one hypothesis is appropriate, and that agreeing with the other hypothesis inappropriate. In such circumstances, he who should choose to live as though he knew the future life to be a fact, would show faith in the future life. Conversely, he who should

live as though he knew that there is no future
life would exhibit a negative faith.   Our faith
is shown by our works, and its own inner
essence is the choice of alternatives in the
presence of uncertainty of the outcome.
Faith does not consist in making assertions,
but in adjusting life to a hypothesis, or even to
a hope.   One's faith is precisely identical
with the hypothesis or the hope which the life
practically expresses.   It may be either positive
or negative, religious or irreligious.

Such is the function of faith in its relation
to certainty and uncertainty.   It does not consist in becoming convinced of a creed which
reason is unable to decide for; it does not
consist in finding out that God has forgiven
our sins or regenerated us; it is rather voluntary movement along a particular path of practical living.   But the full breadth and meaning
of faith is not brought out by any consideration of its relation to the intellect alone.
Faith is no mere makeshift to be resorted to
when knowledge fails us. ˙ Like a ship's compass, it is necessary in the clear sunlight of
knowledge as well as in the fog of intellectual
perplexity.   Something of its breadth is reflected in the etymology of the term.   Faith

and fidelity have the same root. Similarly, the Greek verb, through which we are commanded to have faith, though it can have the signification of assent to a proposition, is also applied to having confidence or trust in a person, of relying upon a person or thing, of complying with a demand or request, of obeying, and even of daring something. Faith is the whole process of guiding and forming our life in accord with the life-principles of Jesus. Whoever trusts in God, as Jesus has revealed him, has Christian faith; likewise, he who complies with what Christ has commanded; finally, none the less truly, he who dares to cast away un-Christly ideals and principles and enter upon the life that Christ commands.

A similar problem arises with respect to the love that is called the essence of Christianity. How can I be commanded to love any one? As in the case of repentance, two words having distinctly different meanings in Greek, are translated by the single English word, love. One is the love of fondness, or affection, a matter of emotional inclination; the other is a love that can be chosen, and one that may include self-denial or the restraint of inclination. It consists in loyalty, in service, and in all that is involved in choosing the interests of another as one's own interests.

The two varieties of love may, of course, co-exist, and either one may give birth to the other. Conjugal love, beginning as mutual attachment of the feelings, normally goes on to become also a principle of loyalty adopted by the will and made a controlling factor. Conversely, who does not know how feelings of fondness awaken toward those whom we serve? Experience shows that one who begins the Christian life by loving God in the sense of voluntary loyalty and service is likely sooner or later to find himself impelled to such service by joyous inclination. Nevertheless, though the two kinds of love are thus closely related, they should not be confounded. In one sense of the word, a command to love would involve us in nothing but confusion of mind, but in the other sense such a command is as reasonable as the ideal upon which it is based.

## *The Birth from Above.*

The simplicity of the Christian life-principle has been obscured by still another misfortune of language, namely, by the employment of "born again" to represent Greek terms whose plain, literal meaning is "born from above." We come here to a question somewhat different from those already discussed, inasmuch as the divine side of membership in the kingdom now comes distinctly upon the horizon of our thought. Thus far we have dealt with the act or acts of our own will involved in becoming and continuing disciples of Christ. Now we must recognize that these acts are connected with something higher than our finite selves. The disciple of Christ is one who is born from above.

It would be easy at this point to undo all the work of clarification that has been attempted in the earlier parts of this chapter. As soon as men come to the question of the new life it seems as if almost always an evil fate pushed them over into dogmatic debate and assertion. Repentance, conversion, faith, and love may all be cleared up and put into practical form for use in Christian living, but the new birth becomes an everyday entanglement. There is no need of denying that it is a subject for profound thought. We face here nothing less than the problem of the ultimate source of moral improvement in individuals and in the race.   There is involved, also, the mystery of the relation between our own freedom of initiative and the co-operation of divine power within the unsounded deeps of our being.   If the practical application of the idea were dependent upon the solution of such questions, or even upon the adoption of an hypothesis regarding some of them, we might well question the wisdom of the formula altogether.   It must be possible to pluck the fruit of Jesus' teaching in some more direct way.

This direct way, as has been intimated, has been concealed by an unfortunate translation.   The uncertainty that afflicts many a conscientious soul, and that blocks the way of many an inquirer, will not be removed until we candidly substitute "from above" for "again."   We are to be born from above. That which is of the flesh is flesh, and that which is of the spirit is spirit.   The root-contrast here is not between what is before and what is after, but between a higher and a lower.   We have here no question of times and of seasons, of which Nicodemus's nation was strenuously particular, but of the content of the life.   Again, Jesus plainly says that the main question is not the whence and the whither; it is not a question of how a process is wrought, or of process at all, but solely of the contrast between a spiritual and an unspiritual mind.   Our English "born again" has promoted and kept alive a misunderstanding closely parallel to that of Nicodemus. We have been looking for events and disputing about processes.   We have caused men to ask themselves, "Have I been born again? Am I sure that an event has taken place?" whereas, we should have pressed home to them the sharp contrast between a spiritual and an unspiritual content or quality of life. What am I, qualitatively considered?   Am I living the life that is from above, or that which is from below?   That is the essential question for every one of us.   In the absence of the heavenly quality in the life, no experience of internal wonders is valid evidence of the birth from above.   On the other hand, if I am really on the side of Christ, I am born from above, however this comes to be the state of my mind.

The habit of looking for newness instead of for heavenly quality works confusion in two directions.   First, persons who are able to answer the question of dates to their own satisfaction, meet the temptation to substitute a "has been" for an "is." They estimate themselves by something other than the present fact; they would turn the mill with the water that is past. Something of vital power must always be lost when the spiritual life is measured by anything whatever except its own content and its fruits.

Persons of a different make-up suffer from the opposite error. Desiring to dedicate themselves to the Master, yet unable to put their experience of spiritual realities into the forms of book-keeping, they hesitate, postpone action, are harassed by doubts of their personal status. They, too, ask themselves "Have I been?" when they should rather ask "Am I?" They need to be told that whosoever prefers above all things that for which God gave us his Son, and Jesus gave his life, is born from above. The fundamental preference is decisive as to the inner quality, and the fruits are decisive as to the vigor of the inner life. Many reach this point by a sharply marked transition from rebellion or indifference. Others find themselves, they hardly know how, gradually becoming satisfied with what satisfied Jesus, and dissatisfied with what displeased him. Some feel that a power not themselves supersedes their faculties and makes them over new. Others are more conscious of the influence of their own deliberation, choice, and effort. Finally, some, who should be counted happiest of all, have never known a negative period. Taught from infancy to count themselves the Lord's, they have never had any other fundamental preference. Whoever belongs to any of these classes has a right to say that he is born from above, that he is a child of God.

But, it will be asked, what becomes, then, of the notions of a new heart, the work of the Holy Spirit, the witness of the Spirit, and in fact, the whole miraculous part of the process? Let us answer these questions in order. The new heart, that is, the heart that has the life from above, is found wherever there is one who prefers the things that Jesus loved. The new heart is to be defined by its quality, not by its history. And what do we mean by the heart, if not that out of which are the issues of life? A man's fundamental preference defines the quality of his heart. This is a matter of the whole man; he judges all

things by the Christian standard, he feels
drawn toward the things that it approves, and
he chooses them as his good.   Impulse may
play a larger or a smaller part, according to
the temperament.   Happy the man whose
spontaneous tendencies have all been brought
into subjection to the Christ!   But that is the
consummation rather than the beginning or
the middle of the life from above.   There are
all degrees of immaturity, spiritual as well as
bodily, and the phenomena of growth vary
from individual to individual.   One proceeds
smoothly and regularly from stage to stage
without marked emotional transitions; others
experience rapid unfoldings from time to time,
marked by emotional concentration and explo-
sion.   The former have a less dramatic experience, but the latter suffer reactions from
their emotional exaltation.   Yet the essential
fact is the same in both cases, namely, a
fundamental preference, to which the habits
and feelings and spontaneous impulses become
more or less gradually conformed.

But what about the work of the Holy
Spirit, and where comes in the divine hand?
Any complete answer to this question would
carry us far beyond the limits that have been

set to this discussion. It is fitting, however, to say that no defensible theory of divine influences in the mind of man has been interfered with in the slightest degree by what has been said. We have not excluded such influences from the facts under consideration, but have simply declined to enter upon the philosophical question of where the human ends and the divine begins. Let us grant that God is in it all from beginning to end. If, then, one should demand to know where the divine element is to be found, an answer might be framed on the model of the famous epitaph of Sir Christopher Wren, the architect of St. Paul's cathedral; inscribed over one of the portals of that noble edifice are the words, "If you are looking for his monument, look about you!" If you ask, "Where is the divine hand manifested in a life whose fundamental preference is Christlike?" the answer is, "Look about you." The evidence of divine workmanship is qualitative. God is love, and he who dwells in love dwells in God.

*We Must Claim Our Citizenship.*

How hard it is for creatures of sense to measure spiritual things by spiritual stan-

dards.   We will obey God, or acknowledge his
presence in our lives if, forsooth, he will only
send a messenger from the dead, or smite our
senses or our emotions in some phenomenal
and mysterious manner.   We will count ourselves disciples, provided he will issue to each
of us a supernatural diploma, certifying his
state of mind!   Yet the very persons who
thus insist that God should come out of the
clouds by some miraculous attestation addressed to us personally, confess that no man
has ever yet seen God, but that the Son has
declared him.

Why not be in earnest with our belief that
God is revealed in Christ?   Do we wish to
know what God thinks about us?   That is
precisely what Jesus has come to reveal; that
is the Christian revelation.   We are not to be
forever crying out, ''Show us the Father!''
but rather, taking Jesus at his word as to the
disposition of God toward us, and as to our
privilege of being his children, we are to make
him our choice, and immediately proceed to
work with him, claiming our right as children
of God and citizens of the kingdom.

John has summed up the whole matter for
us in a few swift words: ''To as many as

received him (the Logos) gave he power (or authority, or the right) to be called sons of God.'' This is personal religion. It is direct commerce of the soul with the ultimate verities. The willing soul needs not to wait for verification from priest or scribe, or even the annals of his own heart. Let him call himself by that glorious name of son, and let him rejoice in the grace of God.

Whoever thus receives Christ by assimilation of one's fundamental choice with his, will discover that the whole nature is being molded in accordance therewith. There will come into the feelings some sense of harmony between one's own life and the primary conditions of life. You may call this a good conscience, or you may call it the witness of the Spirit, or you may leave it a nameless joy—in any case, this inner unity of ourselves with ourselves, and this sense of being at home in God's presence, appears to be just what Jesus promised when he said that he and the Father would come in and sup with us.

Our talk has been chiefly of the relation of our will to the conditions of Christian discipleship. But we must not undervalue the emotional satisfactions that come into the

Christian life in proportion to its development, and in accordance with the temperament of the individual. We need not apologize for strong religious emotion, or for aspiring to what used to be described as "enjoying religion." It is necessary, however, to insist that emotional experiences are not a condition of entering upon the Christian life; that they are not the essence of piety, nor the test of it, nor the primary and essential evidence of discipleship, nor the goal of Christian living. The conditions, the essence, and the test of discipleship have reference to our relation to Jesus' great concern, the kingdom of God. Whoever can honestly pray the Lord's prayer, in the sense that Jesus obviously gave to it, is a Christian.

# THE BREADTH OF RELIGIOUS EXPERIENCE

# CHAPTER VIII

## THE BREADTH OF RELIGIOUS EXPERIENCE

Theology has begun the twentieth century committed to the doctrine of the immanence of God. If this doctrine is true, it should find illustration and confirmation in religious experience. If God is ever present in all nature and in the soul of man as the living source whence their very being springs, then all our dealings with ourselves and with nature involve some sort of commerce with Deity. In that case we need but become aware of things as they are and of ourselves as we are in order to find religious experience broadening out far beyond the special group of facts to which that term is ordinarily applied.

### The Influence of Mysticism upon Modern Religious Life.

Curiously enough, the historical movement whose logical affinity is for experience in this large sense has in our day become insistent upon a small group of special phenomena which practically usurp the name of religious experience. In popular parlance this term has come to signify conversion phenomena, with the addition, possibly, of assurance or witness of the Spirit, and some more or less occasional states of divine communion or instances of divine help. These are the modern substitute for and successor of the ecstasy and similar states of mediæval mystics.

To say that mysticism in both its earlier and its later phases presents only an imperfect exposition of the Christian's privilege of a conscious, personal relationship to God, is not to ignore its immeasurable service to vital, as distinguished from formal, dogmatic or ecclesiastical piety. In mysticism the heart found a voice. It declared that true religion is inner life rather than outward observance, experience rather than inference, direct and conscious contact with God rather than ecclesiastical enginery. It was the salt of the mediæval church, and the Reformation movement came largely out of it. No small part of the power of Protestantism has been the power of a personal experience. Nor is it too much to say that vital progress at the present stage depends upon our discovering how to unite ethical endeavor with personal communion with God, or rather upon our finding that the outward and the inward sides are one and inseparable.

Yet we ought not to conceal the fact that mysticism has been based very largely upon misunderstandings. It justified itself in part by the Scriptures, particularly by the trance of Paul, in which he was caught up into the third heaven, and heard things that it is unlawful for a man to utter. But it was derived chiefly from a heathen source. It adopted into Christianity the practices of the Greek and other Neo-Platonists. Neo-Platonism, in turn, derived these practices from the East. To this day, Indian mystics are endeavoring to overpass the bounds of body and of self, and thus to mingle their being with the being of God. Christian mysticism, in its extreme form, adopted these very processes, and by trance or ecstasy, visions or revelations, sought immediate communion with the divine.

Distrust gradually tempered these excesses, yet their mystery remained. They appeared to be full of supernatural meaning, but later developments of psychology have dispelled the mystery also. The trance of the mystic religionist, like that of the spiritualistic medium, is simply a state of self-hypnosis, in which the subject's mind is almost wholly given over to imagination and emotion. The position of this whole series of phenomena is so well determined that we can produce them at will under favorable conditions.

Mystical experiences had milder forms, of course, shading all the way down from ecstasy to the comfortable feeling that accompanies steady contemplation of the thought of God. It is also true that the stream of Christian mysticism has largely purified itself of the errors that it derived from its heathen source. Yet we should be unduly sanguine if we should suppose that all harmful misunderstandings arising from this source have been removed from Christian thought and practice. There is still among us a disposition to seek God, where the heathen seek him, in signs and wonders, though Jesus declared this to be the tendency of an evil and adulterous generation.

A mistaken notion of human faculties is another of the legacies from Neo-Platonism. Plotinus regarded the soul as threefold—the animal or sensuous soul, the logical or rational soul, and what we may call the spiritual soul. Christian mystics sometimes said that the soul has three eyes, sometimes that it has two. Several writers represented the spiritual faculty as a spark of the divine life within the human. All these views agree in separating the religious faculty from the rest of the mind. In a parallel way we, too, talk about the spiritual nature or faculty as though it were something specifically different from the faculties with which we attend to life's ordinary business.

To modern psychology, of course, the soul is not a collection of faculties, each of which functions by and for itself. The so-called spiritual nature is simply the mind employed about religious matters, as at other times it is employed with other concerns. Yet, do we not live as though the religious part of us were stored away in some garret room of our nature, apart from our everyday employments? This notion of a division of our personality finds one expression in the theory of the Roman Church, that the spiritual life is a specialty of experts. The "religious," in its parlance, are those who devote themselves to

God as monks, nuns, and priests. The same misconception reappears in the distinction between the sacred and the secular. When a man prominent in public life asks what the Ten Commandments and the Sermon on the Mount have to do with practical politics, we meet an extreme, though not surprising, application of the same idea. How would it affect the men and women of to-day if the truth should once take possession of their minds that the faculties with which they worship on Sunday are the very same ones with which on Monday they go about their so-called worldly occupations?

Closely connected with the misunderstanding of human faculties is the notion that religious experiences are merely occasional events, that they are the luxuries rather than the staple of religious living. Porphyry says that, during the six years that he spent in intimate relations with Plotinus, the latter experienced union with God only four times. So, some modern Christians seem to think it sufficient to have come only once or twice into a clear sense of the presence of God.

Not all mystics, however, can be charged with this occasionalism. A curious example of a higher type is Brother Lawrence, a Carmelite monk at Paris two hundred years ago. He declared that, "the most excellent method he had found of going to God was that of doing our common business without any view of pleasing men, and (as far as we are capable) purely for the love of God. That it was a great delusion to think that the time of prayer ought to differ from other times; that we are as strictly obliged to adhere to God by action in the time of action as by prayer in the time of prayer." Brother Lawrence, not being a learned man, had been set to work in the kitchen of the monastery. He says of his occupation there, "The time of business does not with me differ from the time of prayer; and in the noise and clatter of my kitchen, while several persons are at the same time calling for different things, I possess God in as great tranquility as if I were upon my knees at the blessed sacrament." (See "The Practice of the Presence of God." New York and Chicago: A. H. Revell.)

Not only are such experiences possible, but reliance upon the merely extraordinary phenomena involves specific dangers. In order to illustrate this insecurity, and at the same time to show something of the actual range of religious experiences, I shall quote largely from accounts of such experiences now in my possession.

## Visions, Voices, Inspirations.

It is certain, in the first place, that we have among us many persons whose experiences occasionally approach the standard set by the extreme mystics. Here are three examples:

A young man who had felt called to preach, and had resisted the impression, had gone to work in a mine. "One night," he says, "while working on the three-hundred-foot level of the . . . . mine, running a car of waste, I heard a voice which said, 'John, John, I have a work for you to do!' Heart-stricken and penitent, I fell on my knees, and in the silence consecrated myself to God. . . . . The voice that I heard in the mine I seemed to hear with my natural ears."

Another young man, while following the plow, "suddenly heard a voice in articulate speech say, 'Go and prepare yourself for my work!' I was probably more than half a mile from home, and so far as I know, from any living human being. I stopped my team with one sudden jerk and looked around, expecting to see some one, but no one was in sight. But, just before me, suspended in the air, it seemed to me I could see the map of Africa, though for what reason I never could tell. The next thing I knew, I had been upon my knees for some time pleading with God not to make me preach."

A third young man, while struggling with the problem of how to believe on Jesus, instantly had a vision. He says: "Whether in the body or out of the body, I cannot tell; God knoweth. I saw two persons smiling upon me in the deep, blue sky. O, such faces of tranquility and peacefulness! It seemed to transform the restless, agitated atmosphere around my poor soul into a peace like theirs. It vanished. I went out and in wondering. I was in a company, for I knew it."

Closely related to such visions and voices are modern inspirations. Speaking of certain experiences connected with his sermons and orations, Henry Ward Beecher said: "There are times when it is not I that is talking; when I am caught up and carried away so that I know not whether I am in the body or out of the body; when I think things in the pulpit that I could never think in the study; and when I have feelings that are so different from any that belong to the lower or normal condition that I can neither regulate them nor understand them. I see things and I hear sounds, and seem, if not in the seventh heaven, yet in a condition that leads me to apprehend what Paul said, that he heard things which it was not possible for a man to utter.'' ("Beecher's Patriotic Addresses." Edited by J. R. Howard, New York, 1887, p. 140.)

By a similar process Horace Bushnell reached the solution of certain theological problems. His biographer, Munger, says: "On an early February morning his wife awoke to hear that the light for which he had waited had come. She asked, 'What have you seen?' He replied, 'The Gospel!' It came to him at last, not as something reasoned out, but as an inspiration—a revelation from the mind of God himself. . . . . He regarded this experience as a personal discovery of Christ and of God as represented in him. He himself explains it: 'I seemed to pass a boundary. I had never been very legal in my Christian life, but now I passed from these partial seeings, glimpses, doubts, into a clearer knowledge of God and into his inspirations, which I have never wholly lost.' '' (''Horace Bushnell, Preacher and Theologian.'' Boston, 1899, pp. 113-115.)

## A Contrasting Type of Religious Life.

The cases just cited may stand as representatives of the whole large class of persons who realize a sense of God's presence through some process in which, as it appears to them, their faculties cease to operate in the normal fashion, and come under the control of a superior power. Other persons, whose religiousness is unquestionable, never have any such phenomenal manifestations. God is very real in their lives, and yet they are unable to point to a single experience which does not seem to them to fall under the ordinary laws of the mind. Three cases may be cited by way of illustration. One is that of a young man who has devoted himself to foreign missions, and the other two are cases of clergymen in the home field.

One of the three writes: ''I should have great hesitation in laying claim to any real, tangible witness of God's presence, although

I covet such a blessing greatly, and have prayed earnestly that I might share in those definite experiences of which Christians often speak. I have felt in my inmost self a sense of approval when I have done right, a sense of condemnation when I have done wrong, but I cannot say that this has been more than any conscientious moral man daily experiences.''

The second says: ''I have striven to come into immediate communion with God, to have a sense of his presence, but that has never been. He seems at such times not far away, and yet never sensibly present. He seems just to elude me. More and more I enjoy the quiet hour, love more and more to read devotional literature, . . . . but in none of these is there an immediate sense of God's presence. . . . . I have had a long, bitter experience because of the language of people at revival meetings, etc. At times I have felt that I was not religious as I ought to be, or rather that I had no religion whatsoever.''

One noteworthy feature of this case is the enjoyment of what is called, in the technical language of the mystics, ''the contemplative life.'' Religious satisfactions are found, in increasing measure, in the reading of devotional literature, and in quiet contemplation. This is one of the precise processes whereby persons of the mystical temperament secure a clear consciousness of the divine presence. It is a fair question whether the psychological fact is not the same in both cases, the great apparent variance being merely one of interpretation or of theoretical statement.   May it not be that the mystic's sense of God's immediate presence is identical with the enjoyment of "the quiet hour" to which the writer just quoted refers?   The mystic merely objectifies and accepts as divine what the other, more analytical mind, tends to refer to its natural causes.   Perhaps both are right.

A third report says: "I do not seem to be able, so to speak, to lay my spiritual hand on him and feel his electrical touch.   I believe that he rules and overrules in my life, . . . . and yet it seems as if I have to be content with receiving God at second hand.   Nature is to me a means of God's revelation of himself, . . . . as also man, with his divine faculties and powers. . . . . The chief revelation of the goodness, wisdom, and love of God to me is in Jesus Christ.   Jesus is more real, personal, and helpful to me than any other influence of which I am conscious. Only the phrase, 'loving, vital union,' can express this relationship. It has come to be what it is chiefly through three direct sources of experience: first, through seeking to arrive at a full and accurate concept of him; second, through an inner desire to become useful and Christlike; third, through a desire to know, love, and help all persons whom I may touch. This love for men, passion for souls, is the newest, sweetest, and most promising emotion that has ever possessed my soul.''

This writer has a ''loving, vital union'' with Jesus, in whose service he enjoys the sweetest emotion that ever possessed his soul. Possibly these are the very facts that other persons call immediate experience of God. But, whether this be so or not, we are obliged to face the fact that some devoted souls appear to themselves not to have experienced any such personal revelation. They have seen no visions, heard no voices, enjoyed no ecstatic communion, received no inspirations, been conscious of nothing beyond what they are able to classify under the ordinary workings of the mind.

To say that these men have no religious experience, would exhibit extreme foolishness and bigotry. Nevertheless, it must be confessed that the concept of religious experience, as ordinarily employed, has scant room for such persons. Has not the time come when we should frankly and persistently deny that the culminating type of religious experience, by which all other types are to be judged, is a state in which rational self-control lapses? Is the normal consciousness a Godless one? And is the divine presence to be certified by the unnaturalness (or preternaturalness, or supernaturalness) of a process?

Against this misunderstanding three considerations may be urged. First, many persons are profoundly pious who have no such experiences. Second, modern psychology is rapidly taking out of the realm of mystery the whole class of processes that culminate in ecstasy. They are discovered to follow ordinary mental laws. Third, it can be shown that essentially religious states and experiences accompany or form an element in the normal use of all human faculties.

*All the Strings of the Harp Respond to God's
    Touch.*

The God-consciousness comes to one person through one faculty, to others through
another, and to some through no discoverable
special channel, but rather through the whole
mind in its ordinary occupations.

Here are, first of all, men and women who
confess that the sense of the divine presence
is experienced by them solely through feeling.
"I have no inner voice except feeling," says
one man. "When I do right, it makes me
feel so good or so blessed that I can scarcely
control myself. When I do wrong I can
scarcely sleep for remorse. . . . . So, I am
religious because it makes me happy. . . . .
Men may laugh at Methodist preachers for
working themselves up into a perfect frenzy
and calling it the power of the Holy Ghost,
and I realize that they have grounds for their
criticism, but I would walk five miles any day
I have time, to get into a crowd and be
worked up to such a frenzy. I realize that
my nature forces me in this way, whether
you or any one would admit that it is the
power of God or not. I like to think that

it is, and instead of trying to subdue it, I rejoice in it.''

Compare with this disciple of emotion one of another temperament: ''There has never been in my life anything of the nature of supernatural evidence, and practically nothing commonly called feeling, . . . . yet I know, feel or not feel as I may, that God lives and is the one real, everlasting part of the things that have to do with my life.'' This ''I know,'' which is doubly underscored in the original, means, of course, acquaintance with, not merely theoretical knowledge about.

Other persons find God's presence in their ordinary intellectual processes and pursuits. ''My studies in science,'' says one, ''have most wonderfully increased my sense of God's goodness and power.   Nothing gives me such a sense of the reality of God.''   Another notes the fact that, strangely enough, as it seems to him, he has often had a sense of God's presence at the moment of experiencing doubt on religious matters, and he believes that this fact has kept him back from doubting the existence of God.

The moral nature is the chief avenue through which others receive impressions of the divine presence. "I have prayed for joy and peace," says one, "but these have never come to me unless it was because I had done some hard duty or made a sacrifice. . . . . I have been conscious of his approval and disapproval, but I cannot tell how, or whether it differed from conscience." Another says that, though conscience seems like the voice of another speaking in his soul, he doubts whether he would have regarded it as the voice of God if he had not been taught to do so.

In some cases, the consciousness of God is mediated by the social nature. "In prayer I am conscious of receiving something as well as of yielding up something. The transaction is mutual. . . . . To explain this reciprocal influence is difficult. In quality it is not unlike all satisfaction that comes from mutual kindness between man and man." Again, not seldom the sense of the divine is interfused with the exercise of the social instinct between man and man. "His presence is manifest in me," testifies one, "after having done some little kind deed, or after having spoken a kind word to one distressed or feeble." Not a few persons experience in exalted conversation with their friends what Emerson calls the Over-Soul. Affection between lovers frequently seems to have in it something far transcending the human. "In thine eyes," said a dying man to his wife, "In thine eyes have I beheld the eternal!" I have received several reports of this particular type of experience, but I will quote from only one. "I have never been able," says the writer, "to distinguish the 'love of God' from human love." As a consequence, when he attended a young people's meeting in company with a young lady whom he loved, he was unable to decide whether the emotions aroused in him were of divine or human origin. He was careful, therefore, not to offer his testimony lest he should commit sacrilege by confusing the earthly with the heavenly affection!

Similarly, the beauties of nature and of art open the hearts of some men to what appears to them to be a divine influence. Says one: "A gray autumn day always had a peculiar effect on me, making me realize more than ever the presence of God in nature." Here is a more positive testimony. "Upon rare occasions, when viewing and meditating upon the beauty of nature, a quiet influence of exceeding peace has suddenly taken hold of me, and I have felt as though the Creator actually stood beside me.'' Another says: ''I have glimpses of the divine, and they fill me with an intense yearning which is almost a pain, and yet sweeter than any joy I have ever had. One glimpse came to me one night at the symphony concert, when I lost sight of orchestra and audience, of everything but this sweet sadness in which I seemed to be borne out of myself, and brought face to face with the infinite. I had another distinct experience of this one Sunday morning last summer when sitting alone by the lake shore. The same feeling comes to me when I take the sacrament, and sometimes when, in reading, I am impressed with some noble thought. These distinct impressions are not frequent, and I always recognize in them a revelation of something outside of and far above myself. I am coming more and more to a milder appreciation of the divine in all forms of the good, true, and beautiful, an appreciation quite as genuine, but not so impressive as the specific instances mentioned.''

Not less instructive is the less confident

account that follows: "To be alone in beautiful surroundings, to read a beautiful poem, or to listen to music, especially sad or powerful music, inspires more often than anything else, a feeling of what you call divine presence; at least, it is the highest, purest feeling that I know; indescribable, but most akin to a thrill of aspiration, of longing never to be fulfilled. There is little of joy or happiness in it; at most a sense of peace and reconciliation; often bitterness produced by the contrast of this idealized state (especially music) with reality. Whether this inspiration is of a Divine Being I cannot say, but it must be more than a better self, because so incongruous with the self."

## The Divine Presence in the Commonplace.

There is, in the next place, a class of persons who find the sense of a divine presence so interfused with the normal and ordinary exercise of their minds as not to be able to set the two apart. "My religious experience," says one careful respondent, "has been entirely of a subjective nature. Thus, I have never heard the voice of God, either as coming from outside, or as an inner voice which seems like something apart from myself. I am conscious of the presence of God in the sense that he makes himself known to me through the working of my own mind. Thus, I know the will of God through my own will. . . . . In communing with God, I feel reflexive influences. . . . . I cannot explain this peculiar communion between the divine soul and the human, but the failure to explain it does not make it less real or unreal.''

This pervasiveness of the divine in the commonplace is more characteristic of maturity than it is of youth. One writer remarks: ''The manifestations are not as clear as formerly, yet none the less powerful, for they seem to be more a part of the life and nature.'' ''I have come,'' says another, ''to recognize religion as a part of my nature, and to look upon it as a simple element which in its operations is not unlike any other part of me.'' Another remarks: ''To be religious means to me to feel in any form the presence of the life of God in the soul—thus, in the urgency of duty, in admiration for beauty, order, and law, in aspiration after spiritual (moral) ideals, in love and sympathy.''

Still another testifies that, after striving in

vain to secure special experiences, he has come to the conclusion that God is somehow present in the normal exercise of our faculties. He enjoys what seems to be communion with God, but adds: "In all these experiences I cannot say that I distinctly perceive, or seem to perceive, any purely objective power coming to me or manifesting itself to me. They all seem to be natural functions of my own mind, and the sense of communion which they certainly contain appears to depend upon an imaginative projection of my own feelings. It is, therefore, rather surprising that this sense of communion persists; not only does this view of it not weaken it, but the sense has grown and flourished coincidently with my perception of its naturalness."

We have thus traced the sense of God's presence all the way up from ecstasy, through special experiences, to the everyday employments of the faculties. The moral feelings, the social feelings, the æsthetic feelings, all appear to reveal God. So does the moral will, and so, finally, does the intellect, in its reverential joy in the truth.

This is not speculation, but a description of actual experience. The sense of a divine presence can and does penetrate all human faculties. It is not limited to special occasions, or to moments of exaltation. It is not always called by the name of God, or given recognition as a religious fact. It may conceivably be misleading. But the experience is a fact.

If we look still deeper into these experiences, we shall find ourselves approaching the overwhelming conception that something indistinguishable from a sense of divine presence is a constituent factor in all the higher processes of the mind. We shall perceive that all our dealing with truth is pervaded by a more or less dim sense of an authority within it with which we may have fellowship. We shall find all our dealing with right and wrong suffused with some sense of relationship to a Moral Reality at the center. We shall discover that our human loves outrun their finite objects and attach themselves to what seems like a heart of things. In the beautiful and the sublime we shall have nothing less than what Plato found there, a reminder of the divine world from which we have sprung.

Schleiermacher remarked that religion is the "sum total of all the higher feelings," and that, like holy music, it should uninterruptedly accompany the whole of man's active life. Religion is all this, but it is more than feeling; it is the very center and unity and upward-moving impulse of the whole personality. "The measure of the possession of the religious spirit," says Hamilton W. Mabie, "is the breadth and depth of man's consciousness of God's presence and power in the world; and the measure of a man's faith is his ability to realize God in the world about him; in the forces and forms of nature, in the relationships and occupations of man, in the great and small movements of history." ("Life of the Spirit." New York, 1900.)

In a word, the religious experience is what we should expect it to be if the doctrine of the immanence of God is true.

## Being Religious Without Knowing It.

We should expect, as a consequence, to find fragments of a consciousness of God even in men who do not realize the meaning of it or seek to cultivate it as a religious fact. And such fragments are abundant. In one of his moods John Burroughs declares: "When I look up at the starry heavens at night and reflect upon what it is that I really see there, I am constrained to say, "There is no God." The mind staggers in its attempt to grasp the idea of a being that could do that. It is futile to attempt it. It is not the works of some God that I see there." Yet the same author, in another mood, confesses: "I cannot tell what the simple apparition of the earth and the sky means to me; I think at rare intervals that they have an immense spiritual meaning, altogether unspeakable, and that they are great helps, after all." ("The Light of Day." Boston and New York, 1900. Pp. 64, 224.)

Martineau, speaking of the moral nature, says: "Conscience may act as human, before it is discovered to be divine. To the agent himself its whole history may seem to lie in his own personality and his visible social relations; and it shall nevertheless serve as his oracle, though it be hid from him who it is that utters it." ("A Study of Religion." 2 vols., 2d ed., Oxford, 1900. Vol. I., p. 20.)

Speaking of heroic rescues of miners by their fellow-miners, and of similar deeds of unselfishness, Granger declares: "One who loves his friends with this disinterested love is at the same time a participant, though an un-

conscious one, in the love of God, and is a
Christian without knowing it." ("The Soul of
a Christian." New York, 1900. Pp. 170f.)

Schleiermacher gives a similar interpretation of human loves. He asserts that before
a man can have religion, "he must find
humanity, and this he finds only in love and
through love. This is the reason why the two
are so intimately and inseparably connected;
the longing for love, ever satisfied, yet ever
renewing itself, becomes for him at the same
time religion."

That the intellectual instinct also at its
highest becomes indistinguishable from the
religious is well illustrated by that prince of
pure intellectualism, the late Mr. Huxley,
from whose "Life and Letters" the following
passages have been extracted: "Science
seems to me to teach in the highest and
strongest manner the great truth which is
embodied in the Christian conception of entire
surrender to the will of God. Sit down before
fact as a little child, be prepared to give up
every preconceived notion, follow humbly
wherever and to whatever abysses nature
leads, or you shall learn nothing. I have only
begun to learn content and peace of mind

since I have resolved at all risks to do this."
("Life and Letters." 2 vols., New York,
1900. I, 235.) Again, "In these moments of
self-questioning, when one does not lie even
to one's self, I feel that I can say that it is not
so [that his intellectual work is done for the
sake of honor from men]—that the real pleasure, the true sphere, lies in the feeling of self-
development—in the sense of power and of
growing oneness with the great spirit of
abstract truth." (I., 75.)

This remarkable confession of a sense of
communion with the spirit of truth finds its
most fitting commentary in the words of
Augustine: "Where I found truth, there
found I my God, who is the truth itself."
("Confessions," Bk. X., Ch. 24.) "He who
knows the Truth knows that Light; and he
that knows it knoweth eternity." (Bk. VII.,
Ch. 10.) "Behold, there is he wherever truth
is known. He is within the very heart."
(Bk. IV., Ch. 12.)

Men are religious, then—they have religious experience—whether they know it or
not. Paraphrasing Professor James's words
regarding prayer, we may say that we hear a
great deal about why men should be religious,

but we rarely stop to ask why they are religious. They are religious, first of all, because a sense of the divine is involved in all the higher processes that constitute us men. Religion is primarily instinctive, and therefore involuntary. This is the reason why it remains forever young, though the creeds and institutions in which we voluntarily embody it grow old. This is the reason, also, why men who become alienated from one form of religion almost invariably take up some other, or at least some interest that appeals to the religious instinct. One, having rejected the accepted religion, perhaps on rational grounds, falls victim to some extreme form of mysticism, like spiritualism or theosophy. Another becomes absorbed in some interest of civilization or of culture that awakens enthusiasm or reverence or a sense of communion similar to that of religion. The passion for humanity becomes a substitute for religion with some, or shall we say it becomes a religion? With others love of nature or of art, or the search for truth, or absorption in some occupation that employs the higher faculties, fulfils the same function of responding to the demands of the religious instinct.

Without invitation or choice on our part, this self of our self carries us beyond our merely particular selves and proclaims us members of an invisible and spiritual order.

*Being One's Whole Self.*

We are all religious, but some are not religious enough. Some are neglecting to give this deepest self the means of self-expression. Others are half-hearted or one-sided. Some prefer the lower, merely particular self, with its bounded horizon. It remains for such persons voluntarily to turn their attention to this factor of consciousness so as to make clear what is otherwise obscure, to make complete what is otherwise fragmentary, and to choose such ends in life as satisfy this inevitable God-consciousness. We can choose to listen to the inner voice and to obey it, or by choosing not to listen, we can blunt our sense of it.

Religious work and culture have the task of developing this sense of God until it becomes the commanding factor of the life. We have not to ask men to take into themselves something foreign to their nature. Our invitation is rather this: "Be your whole self! Be completely in earnest with your intellectual sincerity, with your conscientiousness, with your love of fellowmen, with your aspiration for all that is true and beautiful and good, and you will find that a sense of God is the moving spring of the whole!"

Some among us are confused, timid, and non-committal because they do not clearly see how being religious is different from simply living a good life. Others are waiting for some special, phenomenal revelation which shall convey a message not otherwise obtainable. All such persons are like the bird and the fish in the poem.

"'Oh, where is the sea?' cried the fish;"

and

"'Oh, where is the air?' cried the bird!"

Let such men know that the religious experience is not something different from living a good life, but is just living it more abundantly. It is the inmost being of such a life. Let them know that we have not to go up into the heavens to bring God down, or into the depths to bring him up. He is very nigh us. "In him we live and move and have our being." What we need is not an infusion of something that ever was totally outside us, but a complete development of what is already within us. God has not left us without a witness of himself in our very members. Whoever sincerely approves anything that is worthy of approval, whoever is touched by the true, the beautiful, or the good, has within him a germ of the worship of God. What is demanded of us is such a repentance of all that is mean, half-hearted and fragmentary as will let that germ grow toward its source as the trees grow toward the sun. We must permit the religious function of our nature to receive God and to rest in him. We must give it a chance to express itself. We must, finally, obey its dictates until, like the leaven of the parable, it leavens the whole lump of our life.

If some one should ask, "But how can I be sure that this which seems to be the voice of God can be trusted?" The answer is still the same, "Live a complete life!" Worship is so wrought into the fiber of our minds that we need only come to ourselves to find God. Not that the religious experience is a demonstration of the existence of God, or the Christian experience a proof of Christian dogma. Even the experience of the senses, though it reveals the existence of an external world of some kind, does not reveal the ultimate nature of matter. Just so, though the religious experience, in its more developed forms, does seem like an immediate touch of the soul with God, we must not decline to subject it to careful logical analysis in order to see whether the impression of the heart is confirmed by reason. But the impression is primordial. It is what we are, and it is as ineffaceable as reason itself. This fact of a nature constructed as if for God is sufficient basis for a mighty presumption of his existence. In the absence of actual disproof it justifies the belief that in the exercise of our entire higher nature we are actually having direct communion with the Father of our spirits.

It is not improbable that, as the years go by, men will rest more and more calmly upon this assumption. There can be no higher destiny or duty for us than just to be our whole selves. Expressed in terms of theology, this is nothing more than experience of the immanent God. It is at once faith and sight. For the practical effect of faith is that we find ourselves at home where we are by assuming that God is there with us. And what more can seeing do? What we need, and what we are coming to find is the God within the commonplace.

> " From Horeb's bush the Presence spoke
> To earlier faiths and simpler folk;
> But now each bush that sweeps our fence
> Flames with the Awful Immanence ! "

# ARE CONVERSIONS GOING OUT
# OF DATE?

# CHAPTER IX

## ARE CONVERSIONS GOING OUT OF DATE?

The mission of the church is to bring the whole world to Christ. In a broad sense, this may be called converting the world. That it is an undertaking of great magnitude is too obvious to have escaped the attention of any; but its complexity has been to a considerable extent overlooked. There are at least four clearly distinguishable duties included under the single notion of converting the world. First, heathen or non-Christian peoples must be made Christian; second, non-Christian persons in Christian communities must be led to Christ; third, children born in Christian communities must be kept for Christ, and prevented from becoming hostile or indifferent; fourth, Christian believers must be built up in the faith and in the application of Christian principle to all parts of individual and social life.

*How the Meanings and Methods of Conversion Shift.*

Nothing is easier than for workers in one subdivision of the field to suppose that their particular phase of the problem of converting the world is universal, and that their particular methods are adequate to the whole undertaking. The mission of which the church was first conscious was that of carrying the good news of the kingdom to non-Christian peoples. As these included the whole world, it was practically inevitable that a restricted notion of conversion should arise, and that it should seem to contain the whole meaning of the kingdom, in its relation to the world. Primitive evangelism had to be addressed to adults, and they had to be first informed of something as yet unheard of, and then persuaded to acceptance. The earliest catechisms were intended for the information of such persons as were desirous of turning from heathenism or Judaism and receiving Christian baptism. But these catechisms came presently to be employed also for preparing the children of the church for baptism. A device arising in one field of work was thus extended to another field in which the requirements were very different—as different as a child is from an adult, as different as the atmosphere of a Christian home is from that of a heathen home in which the name of Christ has not been heard.

Similar stretchings of methods from an original place in which they may have been highly effective to others in which they are not so clearly needed have been common enough. One of them, in particular, has a close relation to the life of all the Protestant denominations, and especially to the non-ritualistic free churches. Where state and church are one, there is practically no such thing as recruiting the church membership, and comparatively little recognition of a line which separates the members of Christ's spiritual kingdom from outsiders. In ritualistic free churches, again, the membership is recruited chiefly by means of a catechumen's class, or similar agencies. From this point the remaining Protestant churches shade away from confirmation based upon catechetical instruction to the requirement of a distinct personal experience of conversion as a condition of membership.

In churches that tend in the latter direction, it is easy to discern a certain narrowing of historical terms to fit the experiences and the methods of a special group of workers. An "evangelist," for example, is here understood to be one who conducts the very special type of religious service called revival meeting, while "evangelism" has come to be synonymous with holding revivals. "Revival of religion" itself has ceased to have its natural meaning, which is exceedingly broad, and has been restricted to such religious awakenings as express themselves in the particular manner here cultivated. "Conversion," in turn, has acquired, not only in revival churches, but also, to a considerable extent, in popular speech, the connotation of certain internal, emotional experiences. In the absence of explanation as to one's exact meaning one is always likely to be understood to mean by conversion the specific revival type of religious experience.

The merest glance at Christian history will show that this is a case in which a part has been taken for a whole. A present, immediate fact, particularly a fact including emotion, has filled the field of vision to the exclusion of vast realms of fact that lie at a greater distance. Revivals, and the revival type of conversion, are by no means universal in the progress of the kingdom of God. In the New Testament we find no preference given to revivals or to the experiences which they foster. Jesus does not make a clear reference to anything of the sort. Much less does he, either directly or indirectly, command such methods of work or the seeking of such experiences. Among his immediate disciples not one appears to have passed through conversion phenomena of the type under discussion, and only Paul, of all the New Testament characters, stands out as a clear case of the kind.

Paul himself does not appear to have taken his own experience as a standard of conversion. He told the story of it in his own defense, but his ordinary preaching appears to have kept it in the background. There is little if any evidence that he demanded striking conversion phenomena in others, or that he commonly witnessed them in his converts.

Other New Testament experiences were decidedly unlike Paul's. Matthew, hearing Jesus' command to rise and follow, arose and followed. The Ethiopian, as soon as he had been told the good news of the kingdom, requested to be baptized. Zacchæus announces his determination to abandon unrighteous ways, and immediately the Master's own lips proclaim that salvation has come to the tax-gatherer's house. These stories set the conversion experience before us no less truly than does the more striking account of the Damascus road incident. In the case of a very large proportion of the persons whom the New Testament represents as believers, the conversion process is unmentioned. Timothy appears to have grown up a Christian from infancy.

The only New Testament event that seems to bear any close resemblance to what are called revivals, is the occurrence on the day of Pentecost. Here, certainly, were social contagion, with its peculiar emotional and involuntary phenomena. But we may surmise that the staunchest believer in the old-fashioned revival would think twice before consenting to a repetition in our days of manifestations which require a defense against the charge of being drunk with wine. However appropriate these Pentecostal phenomena may have been at the time when they occurred, it is not they, but the conversion of unbelievers, which revivalists probably have in mind when they pray for a return of the power of that remarkable day. Further, there is no sign that the special Pentecostal phenomena were regarded, even in New Testament times, as a normal accompaniment of the Gospel. Paul specifically gives speaking with tongues a low place in his estimate of Christian attainments.

Much the same state of facts that we find in the New Testament is found also in the general history of the church. Revivals (in the modern sense) and the revival type of conversion are far from being dominant or typically Christian. Explosive conversions appear sporadically here and there, and we shall presently see that they are to be expected now and then, because some men, like Paul and Augustine, are foreordained by their mental make-up to experience, at critical moments, extreme contrasts of feeling and other states naturally accompanying them. But, in the absence of organized revival methods, such tendencies come to the surface only occasionally and sporadically. It is true that mystical experiences have been cultivated and frequently attained, yet they have been regarded, not as belonging to initiation into the new life, but rather as a privilege of mature Christians, or of specially gifted and chosen vessels of the Spirit.

It cannot be said, then, that conversions, in the sense which the modern revival has given to this term, furnish any adequate measure of the church's progress in her mission of coverting the world. Only a small minority of the disciples of Christ have entered upon the Christian life in this manner, and there is no reason to expect that revival phenomena can ever become universal, or were, in fact, ever expected to be by the Master himself.

### Revivalism Outgrowing Its Own Limitations.

Nevertheless, in ways that are perfectly natural, and nowise discreditable, some of the most aggressive bodies of Christians have come to look upon conversions in this sense as the altogether desirable sign of the assimilation of the world by the kingdom of Christ. They are jealous of revivalism; they look askance at the historically true proposition that it is only an incident in the total history of the church, and their one prescription for all the spiritual defects of the church tends to be this: A revival of revivalism. We shall see in a little while how this attitude of a part of the church of Christ, wherever it prevails, has affected the relation of Christ's whole church to modern life. Where revival phenomena have been witnessed, and the virtue of revivals has been preached, there the world has tended to accept as the most significant signs of Christian life the visible and audible manifestations of revivals, together with the stories told by converts concerning their inner experiences.

Yet no observant person will claim that the revival movements of the last two centuries, glorious as they have been at times, have demonstrated their ability to become a permanent feature of church work. Revivalism is not only not spreading, it is undergoing an obvious struggle for existence in the very churches that have most cultivated it. The old-fashioned revival, in fact, such as took place under the preaching of Wesley, Whitefield, Edwards, and Finney, has practically disappeared. Revival efforts are still common, to be sure, but they rarely show any close approximation to the older type. The preaching, for the most part, is of a different sort. It emphasizes another set of ideas, it appeals to another set of motives, it expects a different set of results, and it attracts the attention of only a special part of the populace. Profound conviction for sin is less insisted upon, and less frequently experienced. How many persons not yet beyond middle life have ever heard sinners groaning with a sense of their undone condition? How many of us have ever known a whole congregation to be seized with terror as the preacher has thundered about sin and its consequences?

As a result, or, more probably as a cause, of these changed revival methods, there is a marked tendency for the beginning of the new life to be less signalized by emotion. The tragic intensity, the high lights, and the deep shadows of other days are little more than memories cherished by a few of the older members of the churches. More significant still, perhaps, is the decrease of social contagion. The strength of the old-time revival lay largely in the forces of which social psychology takes cognizance. It moved men in masses, stirring a whole congregation, a whole city, a whole state at once. It is now some years since anything suggestive of this has occurred except on a small scale, and for a brief space of time. In short, the revival, and with it the revival type of conversion, are just now perceptibly on the wane. They are in a decidedly precarious condition, and if they ought to be looked upon as the universal method of winning men to Christ, if converting the world is in any large measure identical with producing such conversions, then it is high time that the situation be looked into. In any case, the question is of the utmost seriousness. If this instrument of progress is losing its power, we must see to it that progress itself be not stopped.

A survey of the situation will show that revivalism is not suffering from any hostile incursion from without, but that it is being transformed by its own internal forces. We shall see, consequently, that the fact with which we have to deal is not so much decay as development. This is strikingly shown by the history of the three most recent revival movements of wide extent—the Young Men's Christian Association movement, the Salvation Army movement, and the revival movement led by Mr. Moody.

When the Salvation Army began its invasion of this country, many who longed for a revival that would touch the unchurched masses, suppressing their personal distress at the noisy methods employed, said: "Let us stand and see whether this be not the salvation of the Lord. Who knows but that this is the revival force for which we have waited these many years?" But the merely evangelistic services of the Salvation Army soon became as trite as the more decorous revival meetings of the churches. The leaders of the Army had the wisdom to perceive this tendency early in the movement. They saw that mere revivalism touches the problem of the cities only on its outer edge. As a consequence of this insight, bred of experience, the new evangelistic movement evolved into something broader, the energies of the Army being largely drafted off into various forms of social service.

The Young Men's Christian Association movement has gone through parallel cycles of life. The founder, George Williams, was primarily interested in direct spiritual work for the unchurched young men in certain London business houses. Meetings for religious conference and Bible study began the movement. But it was scarcely started before the social and intellectual privations of these same young men forced the associations to provide social privileges, libraries, and lectures. Later came the gymnasium and athletics in response to the inexorable need of city young men. At first these added functions were justified as means for securing the conversion of young men, or for holding them to their Christian profession. But, however much these devices may have done in this direction, it cannot be claimed that they have been an appreciable factor in promoting such revivals as were aimed at. These institutional activities are coming to be justified for what they are in themselves as a needed social service. They are Christian because they perform Christian service and because they maintain the Christian standard of manhood. In the large sense in which converting the world consists in assimilating men in body, mind, and morals to the Christian ideal, these new forms of service are helping to convert the world.

A still more remarkable history is that of

the Moody revival movement, for here we see a great and successful leader, after experience with revival methods, deliberately supplementing them by other forms of Christian activity, while his imitators, following only the former, quickly exhaust their resources. We are still too near to Mr. Moody's person to justify any confidence that we can place him or his work in just historical perspective. Yet a few facts stand out in sharp definition. The first is, that this greatest of recent revival movements departed in important respects from the revival movements that preceded it. Its dogmatic bias was less marked, it appealed less to fear and more to the distinctively ethical motives, and it brought forth correspondingly little of the extreme forms of emotionality. A second great fact is, that in the midst of his successes Mr. Moody discovered the necessity of plowing more deeply than public meetings could possibly do. He therefore turned his chief attention for the remainder of his life to certain educational features of the work of converting the world. This is a remarkable case of adaptation, and it forbids us to think of Mr. Moody as a mere revivalist. He did, indeed, possess in extraordinary degree the qualities of a leader of popular assemblies. He enjoyed the confidence of the churches, so that his work was not limited to any sect. He had a hearing, and an adequate opportunity to show what revivalism of the highest type can do under circumstances now prevailing. Yet, though multitudes heard him gladly, and many were awakened, though the success of the movement was unquestioned, nevertheless, at the summit of his powers, Mr. Moody himself recognized the limitations of his methods. He perceived that evangelism is only one factor in the conversion of the world, and that the slow, painstaking processes of instruction and training are also included. That he devoted most of his strength for the remainder of his life to educational work, therefore, does not indicate any surrender of evangelistic ideals, but only a capacity for adaptation as beautiful as it is rare, a comprehensiveness of vision that multiplies his claims to be called great.

In order to see the inner meaning of the Moody revival movement, we should, perhaps, associate the name of Henry Drummond with that of Mr. Moody. Drummond effected in his own person and in the results of his

work a combination which most persons regard as difficult, and many as impossible—
the combination of intellectual enthusiasm
with spiritual warmth.    It is significant that
college students gave a warm welcome to both
Drummond and Moody, though only the
former was able to approach a student's problems from the standpoint of university experience.    The fact is that both felt the same
need.    The one moved from the standpoint
of culture toward that of spiritual experience,
while the other, starting with the spiritual
experience, strove to add the element of
knowledge and training.

Thus the revival outgrew itself even in its
successes.    Meanwhile, lesser leaders who
have striven to follow in Moody's footsteps, by
carrying on mere evangelism, have found themselves uselessly resisting a receding tide.
The influence of Moody and Drummond, or
of the spiritual current which they represent,
goes on with increasing strength, and it is
nowhere more evident than in the new spiritual
tone of the colleges and universities.    But the
effort to maintain mere evangelism has resulted
in next to nothing except a deep and growing
conviction of its ineffectiveness.    Evangelists

themselves recognize the decay of their influence, and some of them are looking for scapegoats upon which to lay the blame. Some fix the blame for their own loss of power upon the theological seminaries. They seriously believe that the employment of the methods of the higher criticism has paralyzed evangelism. Others find the cause in our material prosperity, or in some other incident of the times. Almost anything that occurs coincidently with the effect is seized upon as a probable cause. What all these complaints fail to recognize is that the present state of evangelism has developed from within evangelism itself. Revival methods have had a fair and full trial. That they have been highly effective in other days no one will deny, but through their very effectiveness they have created a demand to go forward. If they have rendered mere formalism, mere ritualism, mere conformity an impossible interpretation of the Christian life to vast numbers of men and women; if they have awakened an appreciation of the inner life of the Christian, and of the privileges of conscious communion with God, they have also quickened the conscience until men cannot rest in mere inner experiences, mere personal salvation, however self-satisfying.

To the revival quickening itself, then, is due something of the severity with which the revival is being brought to Christ's test, "By their fruits ye shall know them." The revival has had something to do with opening men's eyes to the greatness of the problem of winning the whole world to Christ, and it has made men sensitive toward the manifold woes, the manifold demands for Christly service, which were never seriously, or at least practically, contemplated in the revival program. Once more, then, what we face is not so much decay as development. Those who have the greatest appreciation of the revival ought to be the first to perceive this fact. They should reflect, also, upon the probable effect of reiterating the statement that the new modes of Christian thought, particularly about the Bible, are incompatible with revivals. The friends of revivals should be prompt to deny the possibility of such an issue. The best strategical ground for them would be to assert that the revival has sufficient capacity for inner growth to adapt it to all changes of circumstances.

## Is the Day of Popular Religious Movements Past?

There does not appear to be any sufficient ground for supposing that the day of popular religious movements is past. What is clear is simply that such movements will change in form, in motive, in manifestation, in point of attack, with the general historical development. Men have by no means ceased to move in masses, impelled by social contagion. They are thus moving in many matters. New slang expressions, new fashions in dress, new forms of recreation—bicycling, for instance—new works of fiction, new political ideas, new national aspirations, new attachments or aversions to the person of a leader— such things sweep over the country, carrying a whole people before them, only to be worn out, uninteresting, forgotten in a year or two or three. Recent national conventions of both leading political parties show that men can still be moved in a crowd by a sudden wave of emotional excitement. If mass movements occur at the present time less through public assemblages and more through the dissemination of printed information and incitement, they occur none the less truly. Why should they not take place in matters of religion as well as anything else? What is to hinder wave after wave of religious awakening—of emotion, aspiration, resolve, and act?

Yet it is reasonably certain that such religious waves, if they do arise, will exhibit important differences from the revivals of the past. The reason for thinking so is the changed conditions under which the Gospel has to work. First, the conscience of to-day judges the issues of life by a different standard from that to which the typical revival has made its appeal. The typical revival has worked primarily upon the individualistic motive of desire for personal salvation. It is startling to a modern conscience to read the appeals that used to be made to merely self-regarding considerations. The egoistic point of view was assumed as a matter of course. It was taken for granted that the ultimate reason why we do anything is that we may reap some personal advantage therefrom. As a consequence, the emotions that were commonly aroused were of the sort that existed in full bloom before the social virtues were much developed. The great characteristic emotions of our time, which have to do with social relationships, were awakened only incidentally, or by way of consequence.

Another reason for concluding that the religious movements of the future will exhibit a new type is that the modern mind, as we saw in the first chapter, puts more searchingly than ever before the question of practical utility. Can you show, by the effects in the life, by the influence upon society, that the revival type of conversion has any advantage over other forms of religious expression? Unless such a demonstration be set forth, men will not be persuaded to return to the olden ways. They will always be interested in striking conversion phenomena, but as something to talk about rather than as something that vitally concerns human life. Such a demonstration, it is needless to argue, has not yet been made. The recipient of old-fashioned conversion experiences finds them, of course, of inestimable worth to himself. You will rarely convince such a man that they are not the best thing that life has to offer. But this personal sense of value can be communicated in a convincing way only through conduct.

A third reason for believing that the old-fashioned revival cannot be reinstated, is the clearing up that is taking place in men's ideas concerning the relation of obscure or striking mental facts to the supernatural. There can be no reasonable doubt that much of the power of the old-time revival rested upon the supernatural interpretation which the popular mind gave to certain mental phenomena just because they were mysterious and awe-inspiring. The tendency to look upon the unusual and the mysterious as signs of another world impinging upon our own, is not limited to religious facts, but is found throughout the realm of mental and physical wonders. Only a short way back in our history, a cow or a pig that was taken sick without apparent cause was thought to be bewitched. Men and women were condemned to death at Salem because just such facts had occurred. When the butter refused to come by churning, our grandmothers used to cast a hot horseshoe into the churn to burn out the witch! How much more vividly did mysterious inner experiences seem to be a work of spirits or of God. A strange dream, a waking vision, a trance, started the shivers which we call superstitious. Such phenomena, and others like them, occurring in connection with a revival, were taken as sure signs of divine or demoniac power. Similarly, the sudden reversals of feeling, the spiritual illuminations, and the changed impulses that occurred in converts were taken, because they were mysterious, to be certain proof of regenerative power.

This attitude of mind is passing away. It has not disappeared, to be sure. Whole cults still arise directly out of a parallel interpretation of striking or obscure facts in the mental or physical life. Almost any one, too, feels a little shortness of breath when he comes against a fact, the grounds of which are entirely hidden from him. Nevertheless, through the influence of scientific method, this attitude of mind is certainly passing away.

We are coming to ask for another kind of evidence of the divine presence, namely, godlike qualities of heart and of conduct. We recognize the divine hand in anything that is worthy to be regarded as divine handiwork, and nowhere else. It is true, of course, that such evidence was displayed in the old-time revival. Bad men were made good; wrongs were righted; men's choices were permanently turned to the higher things, and hearts at war with God were brought into communion with him. No slur upon the old-fashioned revival is implied, therefore, when we say that conditions that once favored it are passing away. The great movements of the past performed their own mission to the times and the communities in which they occurred. But it is equally true that present conditions do not favor that particular mode of religious advance.

We may go a step further. Not only does the type of religious revival depend upon historical conditions, but the probability of the revival type of conversion depends at all times upon the make-up of the individual mind. Some persons can, and others cannot, have such experiences. One mind, by reason of its "bent," moves through a series of emotional explosions toward a goal which another reaches by a calm and steady progress. It is useless to debate the question which of these is to be preferred, for such matters do not depend upon preference. Each has something good, too, which the other has not, and each tends toward faults from which the other is relatively free. Neither should prescribe itself as a standard. Nevertheless, if we ask what is *required* of a Christian disciple, we must answer in terms of the cooler experience of willing to do God's will.

Most of the great religious reformers have certainly enjoyed the more explosive type of religious emotion, and to this fact is due, in large measure, the over-valuation that has been placed upon it. The conversion of Saul of Tarsus, in particular, has often supplied to revival evangelism its standard of experience. But what has just been said about types of temperament applies to him as well as to any of us. We are not all Sauls; we cannot all become Pauls. We have not his temperament, or his personal history, or his divine mission. Who can say that the form his conversion took was not as peculiarly Pauline as the mission that was laid upon him? Who shall say that his bringing up, his temperament, his recent persecution of the Christians, the special circumstances of the desert journey, and of the approach to Damascus on an enterprise of blood, did not influence the form of his conversion? The form, not the content. The content, the essential fact, was the change of Saul the persecutor into Paul the preacher.

This is the evidence that God's hand was in the event. How often, in modern revivals, has the form of the Pauline experience failed to be filled with the fruits of the Spirit. But Paul exhibited the fruits, and they constitute the eternal reply to any suspicion that he suffered a mere illusion, an experience without divine significance. The divine presence would have been just as decisively certified, however, if Saul had become a disciple with the calmness of Matthew, Zacchæus, or Timothy.

This, perhaps, is the lesson which a certain depression, not only of revival work but of other forms of religious activity also, should teach us. We have been saying, possibly, that unless we shall see the print of the nails and thrust our hand into the wounded side we will not believe that Christ is with us; while he himself is gently teaching us the faith that finds its complete satisfaction in spiritual values. The process, the machinery, is incidental; what is essential is a Christ-like outcome. In the machinery of Paul's personality we may not all share, but in the outcome, a life filled with the Christly spirit, we may all be partakers. We must be content to be our-

selves. We shall vary, some more, some
less, from the Pauline type, but the same
divine influences are at hand, ready to give us
a mind not merely Pauline, but rather, Christlike. In Paul, and in his peculiar experiences,
what is seen and heard is temporal, but the
spiritual values are eternal.

Undoubtedly this is the real view of the
church of to-day, but the world at large does
not know it, particularly in communities that
have seen much of revival phenomena. There
has grown up confusion of the form with the
content. The simple, plain, common-sense
demands of Christ are obscured. And this
difficulty affects all the churches. For, from
this as well as other causes, there has sprung
up an unofficial religion which refuses to have
anything to do with the churches, or at most
accords them cold approval rather than personal adhesion. The chief ingredient of this
unecclesiastical religion is morality, neigh-
borliness, sympathy, sincerity in human relations. But it is also very often reverent,
even trustful, toward God, and though it
lacks organization, it becomes a real basis of
fellowship between men. It is remarkable
how active the religious instinct is in many

persons of this class. They give ready assent
to doing justly, loving mercy, and walking
humbly with God. They reflect upon the
deep things of life, they experience a sense
of something fitting in the worship of God,
yet they hesitate to ally themselves with the
church because they fancy that some dogmatic
profession or some mystic experience will be
required of them.

## Impending Religious Awakenings.

It is unnecessary to point out further instances of the inability of traditional instruments to move our modern population. Here,
then, is the situation that confronts us: The
capacity, even the tendency, to mass movements abides in humanity; the possible range
and rapidity of such movements have been
enormously increased by the growth of the
press as a means of informing and influencing
men; yet the mass movements in religion,
called revivals, are declining. To make this
picture complete, we ought, perhaps, to call
attention to the variations in revival methods
themselves. Many improvements have been
attempted. Grotesque features have been
lopped off; the message has been simplified

and humanized; individual work has been sys-
tematized; careful planning has been done at
every point. And yet men are not won in
masses.

But this does not imply that the conversion
of the world is halting. The work is only
reorganizing itself. If our eyes had the
spiritual penetration to look beneath statistics
of accessions to the churches, and beyond the
visible aspects of the kingdom to what is actually occurring in the mind of our time, possibly we should see that the converting power
of the Gospel is fully as active and effective
to-day as ever before. Even with our limited vision we can discern some signs that
conversions are not going out of date, and
that revivals, in the proper sense of that term,
are as much adapted to our time as to any
other.

To begin with, the thought of the world is
turning, as never before, to childhood as one
of the key-positions in the whole campaign of
Christianity in the world. Here and there a
movement has begun for the reorganization of
the teaching functions of the church, a movement that is clearly destined to grow and
deepen until it is customary for the churches

to give at least as careful attention to the
religious development of children as the public
schools now give to their intellectual training.
When that time comes, when we actually
apply to the work of Christian nurture the
knowledge and the resources at our command,
we shall witness something more significant
than anything to which the name revival has
ever been given. In the right sense of the term
it will itself be a revival of religion. In the
broad sense, in which it is the business of the
church to convert the world, it will be a work
of conversion; not the conversion of individual
children from rebellion, but the prevention of
a fall from the grace of God vouchsafed to
childhood. But this will involve a transformation of Christendom. It will put a new
song into the mouth of our whole civilization.
The churches will be made over, and the
whole moral and spiritual level of the people
will be raised.

Conversions in this sense are not only not
out of date, they are just about to become a
custom. Think how the way has been prepared for such a movement. Our new
knowledge of the mind, particularly of childhood and youth; the principles of pedagogy

which have so reformed the schools; the growth of a leisure class in the churches, with time, intelligence, and material means at disposal, and restless for something practical to do in religion—these show what might be done, and what, without presumption, we may predict will be done.

Again, many signs point to the approach, from another direction, of a new spiritual enthusiasm. The chief trouble with the traditional revival is that it is not big enough to solve our problems. The motive, the outlook, the program, all are too contracted. Let no one be surprised if the increasing quiescence of this particular kind of religious enthusiasm be followed by an outburst from another crater. "Up from the burning core below" will burst out again, and yet again the primal fire of religion. But the next outburst will be social rather than individualistic, and it will be practical rather than dogmatic or sentimental. It will put sympathy into harness. It will bring a consecration profounder than that of the "consecration meeting," for generalities and vague sentiments will all be swallowed up in practically organizing the whole material and personal power of the world with reference to the kingdom of God. Present wrongs and defects in our social relations are due less to anybody's guilt than they are to a certain immaturity of conscience, which permits us to get wealth first and adjust our account with humanity afterward. Already the conscience of Christendom is out of its swaddling-clothes. It has even reached the sentimental stage of adolescence. It feels the defects of our community life with no little keenness. Presently we shall see it putting into the problems of a Christly organization of society the same energy, foresight, genius for combination, that are now used for the building of great fortunes, and the management of great material enterprises.

This, too, will be a revival of religion, a converting of the world. Even now the motion of its coming can be heard. It makes no statistical exhibit of converts; it has no outward symbol of religious profession; often it does not even bear the name of Christ. But men's hearts are softening toward their fellows, and more and more the conviction grows that the only real measure of life is the measure of Him who went about doing good, telling us to love God and fellow-men. In this revival the church will be converted, rather, is being converted. She is attaining a new point of view, and a new heart. She is not declining, but renewing her youth. She is drawing near to the Master, and from him she is receiving power for greater conquests than ever.

## Converting the World, and Converting the Individual.

No, conversions are not going out of date. But methods are being revised, and points of view are being brought nearer to that of the Master. We can best summarize the whole case by saying that the change through which we are passing concerns the relation of two ideas to each other, the conversion of the world, and the conversion of individuals. Our problem is to accomplish each of these in accomplishing the other. Formerly it was assumed without thought that the only way to convert a community is to convert the individuals in it one by one, and the assumption was further made that each individual is to be moved by individualistic motives. This notion in religion is parallel to the error of the French political thinkers of the eighteenth century who sought the foundation of government in a mere aggregation of the self-seeking wills of individual citizens. We have come to see that the state is no more a secondary product of individuality than the creator thereof, but that society and individual are strictly reciprocal. Each develops normally in the development of the other, and only so.

If, then, the genius of Christianity forbids us to sacrifice the element of personal religious experience by treating men merely as masses, it also forbids us to suppose that the kingdom of God is a mere aggregate of such experiences. Here lies the limitation of the traditional revival scheme. Of course, it would be possible to go to the opposite extreme, as though mere institutions could express humanity. That is a fault of more than one scheme of philanthropy. We must realize that the real world is a world of persons, God, my neighbor, and myself, and that real living can be completed only in communion of all three.

We hear much about serving God by serving humanity. We must go a step beyond that. We must not only serve men, but enter into communion with them, and this communion must include God. This com-

pletion of the social communion in religion
gives the church her specific task in the new
age. She must keep philanthropy and religious experience in indissoluble unity. She
must continue the work of the revival, moving men in masses as before, but by social
motives which include both God and humanity.

Will this new revivalism turn individuals
from sin to righteousness, demonstrating its
regenerating power as decisively as did the
revival that is passing away? Yes, but with
a difference. More sides of a man's nature
will be touched at once, and the tendency to
dramatic climaxes will be correspondingly
lessened. Further, attention will be turned
outward rather than inward, for the very
essence of the social spirit of the Gospel is
that each regards not his own things, but
rather the things of others. Emotion there
will be, but the social emotions will be prominent, and they are gentle and pervasive rather
than explosive. Surgery and purgative medi-
cines will be less in evidence, but wholesome
atmosphere and life in the sunlight of that
love of God which includes the love of men,
and of that love of men which includes the
love of God, will be no less effective. Then,

as always, the wind will blow where it listeth, and we shall hear the sound thereof without knowing whence it comes or whither it goes, but the one Spirit of God will divide to each man severally as he needs.

# SALVATION BY EDUCATION

# CHAPTER X

## SALVATION BY EDUCATION

If the inner history of the relations between Christianity and education could be written—a history that should not only describe institutions and avowed theories, but also reveal the unspoken assumptions and the inarticulate aspirations underlying the whole—it would be a volume of surpassing interest. It would record many a strange fact, many a quaint idea, many a surprising contradiction. The church would appear now as the leading patron of education, now as an opponent or reluctant follower of educational reforms. We should find education pressed upon the young in the name of religion at the same time that the spiritual barrenness of all culture is proclaimed from the housetops. We should find the child held up as a type of the kingdom of God, yet declared to be depraved by nature, and needing to be converted before it can see the kingdom. At almost every point evidence would appear of an internal strain, an unreconciled opposition, between two tendencies. On the one hand, divine grace is exalted in opposition to human nature; on the other, the naturalness of the Christian life is insisted upon. In one of its aspects, Christianity offers, not peace, but a sword; in another, it comes, not to destroy, but to fulfil. When the one phase prevails, education is depreciated; when the other comes to the surface, education becomes one of the chief tasks of the church.

## A Weak Place in the Church's Campaign.

All through this history, however, thus much is plain: The Christian religion has an essential affinity for education. Culture may be distrusted, education may be restricted, faith or the sacraments or divine grace may be emphasized in opposition to mere training, yet one thing Christianity can never do, it cannot let education alone. The debate over salvation by works and salvation by faith may seem to exhaust the alternatives, yet there always remains a backlying assumption that the world's salvation is to be accomplished partly by educating the young.

Is it not strange that salvation by education has never received doctrinal recognition? The churches spend vast sums upon schools and colleges; they maintain Sunday schools at great cost of labor and of gold; they send the schoolmaster side by side with the preacher to heathen lands; yet the principle that governs these things has never been put into words by any official body. We have elaborate theories as to man's part and God's part in other spiritual processes; why not some theory of how God and man co-operate in the education of a soul?

This gap in our theoretical grasp of Christian principles is an index of a serious practical omission. For no one will deny that the weakest point in our campaign for bringing the world to Christ is the relation of the church to the young. Here is our nearest opportunity; here the problems are least complicated, and the difficulties smallest; yet here we are least awake, least aggressive. A hopeful sign of the times, however, is increasing sensitiveness on this point. No sentiment awakens more prompt and universal response throughout the church than the call for reform, or at least improvement, in Christian nurture. Here and there, too, an advance movement has begun, especially in the re-organization of Sunday-school instruction, in the formation of boys' and girls' clubs, and in the efforts of a few leaders to bring the young people's societies into line with known laws of mental and spiritual development.

In the main, however, the thought of the church has not gone beyond, if it has even reached, the standpoint of a certain sentimentality which formulates itself into a few propositions that are too broad to be effective. Thus, it is declared to be wasteful to let the young drift away from the church while we are waiting for them to become mature; that they ought to be held to the church from infancy; that the way to save men is to save boys; and much more. But what it means to "save" a child, or to "hold" him to the church, is not as clear as it ought to be. Hazy notions prevail, too, concerning the relation of a young child's soul to its Creator, and concerning the possible influence of training upon that relation. In particular, the possibility that God should be the prime factor in the education of a child as well as in the conversion of an adult, has found scant lodgment in Christian thought, and meager application in Christian practice. The difference between saving a child and saving an adult has not been distinctly worked out in either theory or practice, and for the most part, the official status of children with respect to the church has been altogether overshadowed by that of adults.

The questions here raised concern the point of view rather than the details of work for the young. Discussions of methods, so much indulged in by workers for the young, are often of little use because they lack a fundamentally correct point of view. They are attempts to walk where there is no ground to stand upon. We shall never do justice to the young until we look down through Sunday-school methods, young people's societies, junior societies, and every mere device, to the ultimate relation in which the three parties concerned—God, the child or youth, and the adult—stand to one another.

Nor is this all. Religious education has relations to general pedagogy that demand to be recognized and applied. The teacher of religion and the teacher of arithmetic are dealing with the same child. Possibly learning arithmetic has something to do with learning to be religious. In any case, the principles of development in the one sphere cannot be altogether separated from those in the other.

In the last chapter the assertion was made that we are now in the first stages of a great religious revival, which takes the direction of the Christian nurture of the young. Let us now try to see what are some of the influences that contribute to this movement, and whither our expectant eyes and efforts should be directed. Our problem is not the old one of "how to bring up children," but rather that of point of view, of attitude, of pedagogical principle.

### How Modern Christianity and Modern Education have Moved toward Each Other.

The way for such a revival has been prepared by a correction of religious ideals on the one hand, and by a correction of the ideals of general education on the other. The result is that religion and education have moved toward a consciousness of a common goal and a common inner principle.

It is true that a merely casual glance does not reveal any such approximation; for no external mark of modern education is more

characteristic than its newly won freedom
from ecclesiastical control. Modern education is, in a sense, distinctly secular. It has
become an institution of civil government.
It is understood to exist for the sake of the
life that now is. It is maintained as a bulwark of the state, a necessity for civilization,
and a means of "getting on in the world."
More and more it becomes practical, relating
itself ever more closely to the everyday life
and occupations of the people. Scarcely a
vestige remains of the other-worldly aspect
which the schoolmen gave to it. No longer
can we assume that any peculiarly close relation exists between learning and the clerical
profession, and if a reason could be found
why the teaching of reading and writing should
be in the hands of the priest, the teaching of
clay modeling, woodworking, cooking, and
sewing clearly lie outside the priestly function!

But when we talk of the secularization of
the schools, we almost always contrast the
school of to-day with the church of yesterday,
the so-called secularism of the present with
the monastic ideals of generations that are
gone. If, however, we compare the ideals of
the new education with those of progressive

Christianity, we discover no such gulf as is commonly supposed to exist. On the contrary, we find something more resembling parallel lines of development. The differentiation of function, whereby education and religion seemed to enter divergent paths, is really tending toward a higher unity of the two. This is another instance in which the breaking up of a germ seems at first to be the destruction of it, when in reality it is merely unfolding into a larger, more varied organism. The unity is still there, but it is a higher unity because it includes diversity and wealth of detail.

For Christianity, too, has been outgrowing the shell from which modern education burst. From the spiritual narrowness which was falsely identified with piety, it has come forth into the light of God's wide creation. To some the church as well as the school has seemed to become secularized; and it would not be strange if some eyes should blink and some feet stumble in the rapid readjustment. But, in general, the secularization that is complained of is of the same kind that Jesus exhibits when, by living a human life, he shows us what God is. More and more we are learning that the Christian life is to be an incarnation, a realization of divine purpose, presence, communion in our everyday occupations. Accordingly, the Christian heart indulges less aspiration to escape the common life, and more to be a whole man, a God-like man, within it. We are not to come down from divine communion to the commonplace, but to raise the commonplace to a sublime level by making it the abode of God.

It follows that the Christian ideal of manhood includes that of "all 'round" development. Every power is to be brought to perfection because every one is a means of incarnating the divine in human life. See, now, how close this Christian view of life is to the ideals of modern education. In both church and school the movement has been toward the recognition of value in the interests and occupations of the common life. In both the one and the other, the ideal of manhood is that of symmetrical development. What religion adds to the modern idea of culture is simply a divine goal and a divine occupation for trained faculties. This is what religion adds, but as far as culture can go in bringing out the powers that belong to a man, the interest of religion is one with that of education.

The bearing of this conclusion upon the general problem of religious pedagogy is exceedingly direct. For education now becomes, not two—religious and secular—but one. There is no ultimate validity in the antithesis that sets religious interests over against secular. There are no religious compartments of the mind divided off from others which are non-religious. There is one personality demanding that all its powers be trained, and there is one sphere of interests in which trained powers are to find use. This sphere of interests, Jesus has taught us to think, is or may be as truly divine as human. The field of the divine life in us is simply our life in its totality.

This thought, like others that have been touched upon in previous chapters, is related to the doctrine of the divine immanence. In whatever our eyes look upon, or our ears listen to, we have to do with God. In all the things that our hands handle, we deal with him. In all our faculties of intellect, of will, of instinct, of conscience, of emotion, we are with and in God. It is as impossible, therefore, to separate religious pedagogy and general pedagogy as it is to expel God from the world which continuously flows from his creative hand.

Education is one, therefore. Some day men will ask what this implies with respect to our so-called secular schools. Already a tide is setting in that is destined to bear us far beyond our present position. Only a few years ago, the public school was assumed to fulfil its function by training and instructing the intellect. But no one who thinks on educational principles at all in this day, has failed to see that the schools must also train their pupils for membership in society. To sharpen the wits without preparing for good citizenship is a foolish undertaking for a state. And so, moral training is now recognized as a necessary part of public education. The schools must aim to make good men and women. Let this movement go a little further, and who knows but that reverence toward God, as well as kindness to animals and good will toward men, will be inculcated in the schools? This might happen, even though church and state remain separate. No doubt any suggestion that religion, in any form, should be taught in the public schools will be looked upon as inopportune, if not wrong in principle. But as surely as the immanent God is the deepest fact of man's mind, progress in the theory of mental development will sooner or later compel recognition of the religious phase as a necessary part of general education.

Until that time comes, the church must make herself a specialist in religious education, and the first condition of her doing so is that she recognize the principles of general pedagogy as being principles, also, of religious nurture. Out of this recognition arises the distinctly modern idea of such nurture. It proposes to utilize, in the interest of religion, the information that general psychology yields concerning the structure of the mind, the information that biology, physiology, and child-study can garner with respect to the laws of child development, and all the principles and methods that the history and philosophy of education have stamped with approval. One of the best results of the modern demand that religion be brought out of the mists and close to life is that the religious training of children shows a tendency to become scientific and businesslike. We should not shrink from applying such terms to sacred matters. If God is to be all and in all, why should not scientific and businesslike methods be the rule rather than the exception in religious undertakings?

## Horace Bushnell as an Educator.

If it were necessary to give a date to mark the transition to the modern conception of Christian training, we could not do better than to name the year 1847, which saw the first issue of Horace Bushnell's *Christian Nurture*. For though Bushnell did not approach his problem from the standpoint of general pedagogy, he had, nevertheless, the insight and the practical wisdom to put himself, perhaps unconsciously, into the central current of the great educational reform of the nineteenth century.

He announced the thesis of his book in the following words: "What is the true idea of Christian education? I answer in the following proposition, which it will be the aim of my argument to establish, viz., *That the child is to grow up a Christian, and never know himself as being otherwise.*" What is this but an application to religious training of the notion of returning to nature out of which sprung the kindergarten, and in fact, the whole modern movement? It is a declaration of freedom from all those mechanical conceptions which looked upon the child as clay waiting to be molded rather than as a life demanding to grow. Bushnell really grasped the idea that the central fact and aim of education is development of a living organism. He therefore assumed the standpoint of the child-consciousness, as modern pedagogy demands, making it, and not maturity, the standard and the guide.

In this year, in which the hundredth anniversary of his birth has been celebrated, it is peculiarly fitting that recognition should be given to the unique place which he holds in the history of education. Horace Bushnell was not merely theologian, preacher, reformer, and prophet, he was also an educator. So directly did he penetrate to foundation principles, that *Christian Nurture* deserves to be perpetually read, not merely out of an historical or antiquarian interest, but because it is a prophetic utterance of a great truth for all time.

That truth has many sides. To do justice

to them all we should have to survey practically the whole field of educational philosophy. But no adequate conception of the place of training in the kingdom of God is possible without at least some attention to the principles upon which he built. Underneath all was the sound point of view of the child-consciousness. It has been the misfortune of the church to form its conception of humanity from adult members of the race, and to conceive of the process of salvation under the limitations thus resulting. We have seen, for example, how the earliest catechisms, which were made for the use of adults, were thoughtlessly assumed to fit the needs of childhood also. This is typical of a long history of the relations of the church to childhood, and it indicates one of the chief causes of our present lack of grip upon the problem and the means of Christian nurture.

Failure to secure the point of view of the child-consciousness wrought havoc in many directions. One of its most obvious results is undue exaltation of the understanding and the deliberate will in religion. Man was defined as the rational animal. He was supposed to base action upon insight, so that the characteristic human formula was supposed to prescribe, first, knowledge of the truth, then conduct in accordance therewith. Hence the catechism and doctrinal instruction became the staple of religious training. The theory was simple and obvious: Let the child first learn the way of life, and then let him choose it for himself.

Such a scheme could never have more than partial success, of course. Even the mature mind seldom reaches its ends by the route of pure theory. How much more is the child-mind a scene of impulse, of fragmentary and unorganized ideas, of particular little inter-ests. Greater wisdom than usually prevails will be necessary if catechisms are to be adapted in any one respect to the mind of the actual child. Such adaptation is possible, but it implies a total reversal of the point of view against which Bushnell reacted. The catechism was bad enough when it was to the child nothing but a set of words to be memo-rized; it was worse when it succeeded in its design of impressing a doctrinal scheme upon the pupil's mind. For now the child took into his bosom the intellectualism which, in one form or another, has long gnawed at the

vitals of our religion.  Whether intellectualism takes the form of orthodox dogmatism, or
of heterodox dogmatism, or of skepticism, it
attacks the inner life of the soul, which is
always more akin to experience than it is to
philosophy.  The real problem of religious
nurture is not that of instilling adult beliefs
into the child-mind, but that of promoting
child-religion in the child-mind.  For this
reason, catechetics must not merely simplify
the doctrines of the church before putting
them before the child, it must abandon the
whole intellectualistic scheme upon which
catechisms have been built.

Bushnell saw that religion goes deeper than
the reason and the deliberate will, which
develop relatively late in life, and that the
spiritual life is strongest when it is most akin
to habit and instinct.  Further, he saw, as
did Aristotle, that virtue need not always be
a product of insight or of deliberate choice,
but that it may grow up as habit and custom
in the moral atmosphere of the family.  The
old theory had been that, at some point, each
child arrives at the "age of discretion," or a
stage of life in which one is responsible for
one's acts.  Before this time, the child was

supposed to lack rational capacity for moral choices, but now he was clothed with such capacity and became subject to all its momentous consequences. The very first use of one's discretion might be an act of disobedience that deserves the divine wrath.

This was the mechanical scheme of thought into which the child was to be compressed. Until the age of discretion was reached, he was left outside the household of faith, or at least in an equivocal relation to it. Children were a religious incubus. Like the American Indians, they were neither citizens nor aliens. They could only wait for religious capacity to arrive, and meantime learn by rote the doctrinal theories upon which they were to act by and by. What Bushnell demanded is, that children be taken altogether out of this equivocal position, given a definite place within the religious organism, and trained as members thereof. It is true that they act from instinct, impulse, imitation, rather than reason; that they cannot understand or accept the doctrines of the church; that they cannot reproduce, even on a small scale, the religious experiences of their elders; nevertheless, they can be truly religious, truly Christian. The imitative, impulsive, habit-forming faculties, in which they are richest, are a proper soil for spiritual seed. Children should breathe in religion as the atmosphere of the home. From the beginning of thought they should think of themselves as belonging to Christ, not as waiting for such a privilege.

Bushnell, therefore, grasped the idea that education is development, and he applied this idea to religion. The child is to be trained not merely *for* religion, but also *in* religion. He cannot receive religion into himself as goods are received into a warehouse, but he can exercise religion, and grow in it as a vital function, like respiration, or sense perception.

The way in which Bushnell herein discovered for himself the central ideas of the great educational reform of the nineteenth century is remarkable. This reform centers about the thought that the child is a developing life, whose internal laws of growth prescribe the principles and methods of education. The child is not a miniature adult, but something qualitatively different. To educate him implies, not that we mold him into conformity to the standpoints and methods of the adult mind, but rather that we provide him with abundant food for his mind, so that he may live out his very own life at each stage of growth. Hence the cry of "freedom in education," which has been heard so often from the lips of modern educators. Free self-expression is the recognized means for the training of the mind as well as of the muscles. The popular statement of this principle is that education does not consist in pouring knowledge into the child, but in drawing out his innate powers. This point of view has necessitated direct observation of the child, and the resulting recognition of relatively distinct stages of growth, each with its own peculiar demands. In principle, Bushnell grasped in original fashion this whole circle of ideas. Religious growth was to be a development from within, not an imposition from without; it was to proceed as spontaneous, unreasoned self-expression rather than as deliberate act; it was to be co-ordinated with the growth of the whole personality.

### Christian Nurture and the Doctrine of Depravity.

Though this is not the place for doctrinal

discussion, we must notice how this modern view of Christian nurture and the doctrine of depravity have already been adjusted to each other. The doctrine of sin can be held in a form that is incompatible with the whole modern notion of education. To wish to develop a child from within by free self-expression assumes value in what the child already is. It presupposes that, somehow or other, there is present at the outset a germ of the highest personality. To the thought of to-day this assumption presents no serious difficulty, for we easily think of God as present in the infant soul throughout its growth, and as being himself the source and inspiration of all good impulses.

Fifty years ago, however, no such point of view could be assumed without challenge. Bushnell, defending his position, felt it necessary to assert that a child may show some really good impulses! Fancy what the reigning view of childhood must have been to call out such a remark! The fact is, that the notion of depravity was the core of the accepted notion of man, children included. The need for religion and the motive to piety were found in the thought of sin. In 1831 the

American Tract Society published a little volume of "Persuasive to Early Piety," which illustrates the whole situation. The book sets out by telling the young reader how depraved he is. The depravity of the nature, it is said, does not infect merely a part of us, but, like a mortal poison, spreads through and pollutes the whole. Even the best actions of one in a state of nature are fatally corrupt. As a consequence, the first foundation of piety is such a sense of our loathsome condition as drives us to accept the plan of salvation. Setting out in this way, the book naturally ends with a frightful description of the torments of literal hell fire. These were "persuasive to early piety" in 1831!

Such assumptions led to training by repression, not by self-expression. Negative rather than positive motives were constantly appealed to. A collection of hymns for children, published as late as 1852, contained such advice as this:

> "Little children, stop and think!
> Turn away from ruin's brink!"

Another hymn in this collection well illustrates the situation which the new views of *Christian Nurture* had to meet. It was printed under the caption, "Motives to Early Piety."

> "Almighty God, thy piercing eye
>     Strikes through the shades of night,
> And our most secret actions lie
>     All open to thy sight.
>
> "There's not a sin that we commit,
>     Or idle word we say,
> But in thy dreadful book 'tis writ,
>     Against the judgment day.
>
> "And must the crimes that I have done
>     Be read and published there?
> Be all exposed before the sun,
>     While men and angels hear?
>
> "Lord, at thy foot ashamed I lie,
>     Upward I dare not look.
> Pardon my sins before I die,
>     And blot them from thy book!"

Bushnell met this state of thought, not by denying any part of the doctrine of sin, but by exalting the grace of God. He simply claimed that the new life, imparted from on high, might and did begin in early childhood. It did not need to wait for the experiences which were common with adult converts. From the ruling notion of depravity itself, in fact, as Bushnell pointed out, it followed that every spark of genuine goodness in a child was an evidence that the new life had actually begun. Thus, without violence to accepted doctrine, a basis was secured for regarding Christian nurture as the unfolding of a spiritual germ present in the child from infancy.

A few years later, another writer, J. G. Hibbard ("The Religion of Childhood." Cincinnati: Poe and Hitchcock, 1864) developed this point extensively by showing from the Scriptures that all children are in a state of regeneration. This state consists not merely in the remission of the penalty due to original sin, but also in a positive gift actually imparted and constituting the new life. This gift, Hibbard maintained, every child retains until, by his own evil choices, he suffers a personal fall from grace. Such a fall is not necessary, and the aim of Christian nurture is to prevent it from becoming a fact, and to develop the germinal life planted in the soul at the beginning. This necessitates a reversal of the notion of conversion. Men had been saying that one cannot be religious until one is converted from Satan to God; Hibbard claims that one cannot be irreligious until one is converted from God to Satan! He supports his theory of universal infant regeneration by calling attention to the belief of his own church, the Methodist, that persons who die in infancy are saved. This implies that they are regenerated in infancy, and it raises the question, Why should infants who die have a privilege that is denied to those who live? In view of the recent declaration of the Presbyterian General Assembly concerning the salvation of persons who die in infancy, this question may be said to be as pertinent to-day as it was forty years ago.

In short, within the lines of the reigning creeds, room has been found for all that the philosophy of education demands. Religious nurture, as well as general education, is development by self-expression. It is the unfolding of a divine germ present from the beginning in the child—personality. It is training within religion, not merely preparation for it.

Here, again, the progress of Christian thought runs parallel to that of educational philosophy. The parallel is well illustrated by the harmony, almost amounting to identity, between the point of view just described and the basal assumptions of Froebel, the chief founder of the kindergarten. Froebel's whole theory is based upon a religious conception of humanity. There is something divine, he declares, in the essence of man, as there is also in external nature, and the purpose of education is to bring the individual to a consciousness of this divine reality, both within him and without. This is the philosophical basis of the beautiful reverence for childhood which the kindergarten inculcates. Under this conception, the child becomes doubly worthy of reverent observation, for now we have not merely to learn by what leverage we may control him, but also how God utters himself within the child-consciousness. Under this assumption, the whole work of education, and not merely its religious part, becomes co-operation with God. The Divine Spirit, by whatever process—possibly physiological and evolutionary—creates those profound impulses and appetences which make us men, while our part is to provide food for them to feed upon.

Indeed, we have only to look beneath the surface to discover that, when religious nurture appropriates the principles of general pedagogy, she merely collects interest upon a loan which modern education has received from religion. The movement for freedom in education, which is strictly correlated with that for civil liberty, assumes the essential dignity of man. It finds within him something worthy of development and of expression. It goes still further, for it sees in essential humanity a proper source of law for the government of men and for the training of the young. But what is it thus to trace ultimate law to man's nature, unless it be to find God there? If democracy is to be more than the collective caprice of the crowd, on the one hand, or more than a fragment of biological machinery, on the other, the deepest fact in the individual must be the presence of the Eternal. So, also, if the mere child is to reveal to us the laws for his own training, this can only be because within the child-soul lives also that Over-Soul which theology calls the immanent God.

## The Present Strategic Necessity.

Salvation by education is a possibility and a fact because education is not merely something that we do to and for the child, and not merely this united with the child's own efforts for himself. God is the central reality of the whole. He is the moving force, the giver of

the inner law, and the goal of all human development. Through education he extends
his saving grace to the child.

This implies that we understand education
in no shallow sense. We may, of course,
exercise one muscle while we permit another
to atrophy, and just so we may train some of
our faculties while others lie dormant, and
this we may mistake for education. But
when education is taken in the profound sense
of bringing to expression that which is deepest
and most real in man, then it becomes a
means of making him conscious of the God in
whom he lives and moves and has his being.
There is a sense in which self-consciousness
may be said to be an end of education, not
the partial self-consciousness that makes one
hypersensitive, introspective and clumsy, or
that which centers one's thoughts upon one's
selfish interests, but the clear recognition of
that wherein one's life really consists. Self-
consciousness of this kind is wholesome. It
may come in various ways—through a sudden
shock that precipitates in an instant all that
life has held in solution; through some profound life-experience, such as love or sorrow;
through a crisis of religious emotion in which

the wood, hay, and stubble of our ambitions are burned up; or it may come through the gentle influences of a training that persistently holds the mind against the realities of its own life. Such training can begin with infancy, and it can continue till old age. It can and does bring men to the obedient recognition of God as the supreme reality, and of Christ as the Way, the Truth, and the Life. This is salvation by education.

Perhaps the greatest strategic opportunity of the church at the present day lies in this direction. Fortunately or unfortunately, the men and women of the western world have become extraordinarily self-conscious. There is probably no precedent for the bold and piercing gaze which they have cast into their own souls. The products are various. The psychological trend of the novel and of the drama; the vogue that pessimism is having; the frequent organization of religious movements upon the strength of some inner experience or mood; the revival of interest in all branches of occultism; much of the feeling and of the philosophy underlying the social and industrial agitations of the day; the prevalent self-questioning with respect to religious beliefs—these all testify to the fact that we live in what might be called the psychological age. Some phases of this movement are expressions of advancing civilization, others are merely ephemeral. But, whether transitory or permanent, the self-consciousness of the age ought to be utilized in the interest of religion.

In preceding chapters an effort has been made to show how Christian faith presents itself as the culmination of self-conscious morality and of self-conscious intellectuality. Being consciously one's whole self in any direction, it has been shown, requires us to assimilate Jesus' attitude toward God. This principle demands to be used, not only in preaching to adults, but also in the education of the young. It is the great fact that makes Christian nurture a possibility in any true and large sense. In all real education, the soul is being unfolded toward God, its source, and its inmost reality.

In spite of the work of men like Bushnell and Hibbard, in spite of the kindergarten movement, in spite of the whole great revival in education, the modern church has never gone at the work of Christian nurture with any such seriousness as the case demands. This work is too commonly regarded as a sort of addendum to church life, and even where it is not so regarded, there is a surprising lack of enterprise in the execution of it. Pedagogical principles cannot even yet secure unequivocal recognition from Sunday school conventions. The methods of the ordinary Sunday school are far behind those of the common school, as far behind as a tallow dip is behind an electric light. In many churches the catechising of children has been largely dropped, and only in a few places has anything taken its place. There is reason to fear that most parents give utterly inadequate attention to religious training within the family. In the minds of many parents, too, there is uncertainty and confusion as to what should be done, or taught, or required, or expected. Meantime, here and there, ''children's evangelists'' and untrained leaders of children's societies and classes ravage the hearts of the young. It would be easy to make a long catalogue of points at which the ordinary handling of children and youth in the name of religion violates known laws of growth and accepted principles of education. And this is the state of our campaign at precisely the point of greatest strategic importance!

Yet we suffer less from defective methods than from neglect. We are not thoroughly awake, and as a consequence, we are tolerant of ways which the slightest reflection would condemn. We must make up our minds to a task not less strenuous, not less systematic and unremitting, than that undertaken by the schools and colleges. This means more than instructing children in doctrine, more than repressing their immature impulses, more than inducing them to imitate the religious habits of their elders—it means the skilful feeding and nurture of the life of the Spirit. The child is to grow up a Christian in a positive sense. Life must be made to mean to him Christian life. This is as far as could well be from all forcing of religious emotion, all precocity, showing off and morbidness. It implies that children are to be mere children, but it implies, also, that the life of every child is a life in God, and that development of the mind should be growth in the God-consciousness.

What this requires in the way of reformed methods, we need not here attempt to say.

When we get the right point of view and are thoroughly awake, we shall discover appropriate methods. But of one thing we may be sure: Any adequate program will require that the religion of us adults become a visible and audible fact, so that children may become aware of its specific presence. Incarnation is the supreme method of Christian nurture. The child must find religion a constant feature of his environment. It must be a perceptible fact in the persons with whom he has to do, and it must enter as a matter of course into his notion of life. You do not have to persuade an American, English, or German boy to have national pride. He acquires it from the unremitting pressure of his environment. Just so, children may be reared under Christian presuppositions so as never to know themselves as being anything but Christian.

We should strive to make this the rule rather than the exception. Christianity must become something other than "a stranger at the door." It must become the presupposition of our family and community life. It must be as pervasive as the atmosphere, as natural as conscience or as love. Only then shall we show the mature and rounded spiritual life that is demanded by the relation of the church to the modern world. Would you have Christian experience come of age? Then give it a childhood and youth.

# THE LIFE OF PRAYER

# CHAPTER XI

## THE LIFE OF PRAYER

Prayer is the heart of religion. When you have told what a man's prayers are like, you have told what his religion is; and nothing more clearly shows the drift of religion in our days than the differences between the way we pray and the way our fathers prayed. The contrast is not a slight one. They agonized in prayer. They wrestled with God. They stormed the gates of heaven, and by sheer violence of desire seized upon the promises and made them a personal possession. We pray with far less assertiveness, with far less confidence in the power of prayer to work specific, tangible effects in the world about us. We question and hesitate where they simply believed. It is highly probable that we spend less time in prayer. Perhaps the fathers were confident because they did not stop to reflect, and we are in doubt because we do. In any case, there is something in our modern modes of thought, our modern attitudes toward religious problems, that involves hesitancy and confusion with respect to prayer.

## Why the Present Confusion and Hesitation?

Realizing this change, our first impulse is to demand a return to the ways of the fathers. But uncertainty of our ground with respect to prayer is precisely what makes such a return impossible until we can see that it is reasonable. Our present duty, therefore, is to diagnose the case, and to seek out the causes of what may be peculiar in our condition.

The present state of prayer among us is a product of practically all the religious, intellectual, and social forces that give a special stamp to modern life.

*First.* In our day, as never before since the voice of Jesus was heard in Galilee, the church is emphasizing service of fellowmen as the true test and measure of piety. Active consecration rather than passive submission has come to be the mark of sanctity, and consecration has come to mean vastly more than any private interchange of soul relationships between the self and God. It consists, rather, in putting the whole self at work upon

the things that God wants to have done.
When we reflect upon the needs of the world,
and upon how God feels toward those needs,
the seeking of any merely personal or private
benefit at God's hand causes us to feel some
secret shame.  In God's order, the world is
to be made over into the kingdom of the
Christ, not by the easy way of begging the
Almighty to do the work, but by the vastly
harder road of doing it ourselves.  The consciousness of this, the mission of every Christian, goes with us to our prayers, and forms
an antithetical background to every petition
for a merely private blessing, to every request
that God will do the work that he has committed to our hands, and to every impulse to
yield ourselves up to the luxury of merely
passive communion.

It is not too much to say that the church
of to-day resembles to a certain degree the
monk of Longfellow's Legend Beautiful.
We seem to be called upon to turn our backs
upon heavenly visions in order that we may
minister to the needs of men.  Of religion in
the form of service we have ever more and
more.  Like the pious monk, we have not
stayed ; but unlike him, perhaps, we have

not yet learned how service rendered to Christ's brethren, instead of removing heavenly visions, may actually prolong them.

*Second.* Along with this emphasis upon service has come a breaking down of the old-fashioned distinction between the sacred and the secular. We have learned that Monday is as holy as Sunday, because all our time belongs to God; that doing the duties of life with hand or with mind is as religious as prayer, because in doing duty we co-operate with God; that, because God is the present basis of all life and reality, he is as near to us in the merchandise we handle as he is in the communion cup, as near to us in the men with whom we do business as in the person of the priest.

The belief in the immanence of God has a wondrous power of dissolving things. Immerse a priest in it, and he comes out just a man among men. Pour it upon the place of prayer and upon the instruments of worship, and all the glamor of special efficacy disappears. Sprinkle it upon the place of business, and behold the partition that separates commerce and industry from communion with God is gone.

Yet in the process of transition from deism and quasi-deism to the doctrine of divine immanence, the thought of God may at first lose in depth at the same time that it gains in breadth. To many persons, no doubt, God is thinned out by the effort to conceive him as truly present in all that is. Just as we are more easily aware of a tree or of a rock than of the all-embracing atmosphere, so undoubtedly the childish notion of God as a particular being apart from other beings takes most ready hold upon the attention of untrained minds. Hence the very act of spiritualizing our conception of God and of the world involves danger of vagueness, and consequent lack of intensity in the sense of personal relationship to the divine.

There is danger, also, that we should level down our idea of prayer instead of leveling up our idea of business. It is true that the doctrine of immanence dissolves many things; but it also contains a supreme constructive principle. It makes more of God in our lives, not less. If, because God is present in all things and in all persons and in all duties, the barriers between business and devotion are broken down, then the affairs of this world, so called, must be leveled up to the standard of prayer. We must recognize God where he actually is; there should be more prayer, not less, and it should be more intense just because it is inseparable from all that is aspiring and strenuous in life.

*Third.* Another cause of the decreasing assertiveness of prayer is the increased emphasis placed by the Christian consciousness upon the fatherhood of God. How many sermons on "Wrestling Jacob" have endeavored to enforce the lesson of "prevailing prayer" by considerations that practically leave out the very heart of Jesus' revelation of the Father. The idea of winning something from God by a contest with him under the figure of the two men who wrestled together till morning, though it may have had religious significance in an earlier stage of religious development, has become impossible to all who have even faintly grasped the bearing of the Christian revelation. God is neither ignorant of our needs, nor indifferent to them. The hairs of our heads are numbered, and not a sparrow falls without his notice. His fatherly care reaches to the whole of human life, from the vast movements of history to the minutest detail of our daily needs. The seeming carelessness of nature is only seeming, for nature and history are both included in one grand scheme of perfect good. As this notion of fatherhood and of providence grows clear, the notion of wrestling with God grows less and less possible.

Our thought of prayer is thus obliged to undergo revision in two directions, in fact. In the childhood of religion, men spontaneously took their own desires as the test and measure of what to pray for, and they supposed that the gods could be awakened from indifference only by sacrifice or insistent pleading. We, on the other hand, know that we cannot find out what is good by consulting our mere desires. We have come to see that the only thing really desirable is that God's loving purpose toward his creation should be fulfilled on earth and in heaven. From this purpose, too, God cannot be swerved by any pressure which we can bring. Now, this consciousness that we have no right to ask for anything except what God is already most interested in doing, simply takes the breath out of much of our would-be supplication. No one with a Christian heart, it is true, can feel anything

but sympathy for a simple believer who urges
God to action, or who, finding an appropriate
promise in the Bible, lays it before the throne
of grace, saying, "O Lord, you've promised
it, and you must keep your promise!" Yet
no Christian with a clear head can fail to see
both the bad logic and the undeveloped spiritual sense manifested in such prayer. It is a
fair question, too, whether many of the persons who have been called "gifted in prayer"
have not won this title by merely revitalizing
tendencies that are essentially sub-Christian.

One reason, then, why the prayer life does
not reach a higher development among us is,
that we still mix these incongruous elements.
We cling to the notion that prayer is essentially asking for something, and yet we feel the
incongruity of begging that God will do the
very thing he wishes to do, and the futility of
begging for anything beyond the range of his
benevolent designs. What we fail to see is,
that the revelation of God's fatherhood for
the first time opens wide before our eyes the
door of prayer. It is an invitation to come
boldly, just as we are, and talk to God about
all that concerns us—our joys and sorrows,
our defects and sins, our duties and aspira-

tions. The begging attitude assumes the
existence of some sort of barrier between
God and the good that is prayed for, a barrier
that only God can remove. But the good
news that Jesus publishes is that no such
barrier exists. If anything stands between
the Father's loving purpose and any good, it
is something in us which we can remove, each
for himself, by an act of his own will.

Thus, the effectiveness of prayer does not
consist in inducing God to do something, but
at most, in removing obstacles that tend to
defeat his loving purpose. Prayer thus becomes not begging, but co-operation. It is
the process of identifying our will and whatever effectiveness we may have in the world
with the will and work of God. This makes
the form of petition inadequate to express the
inner reality and meaning of prayer. It may,
perhaps, serve as a helpful symbol of what
prayer intends to express of dependence, of
trust, of the desire that God's will be done,
and especially of our acceptance of his yearning purpose as our own. Thus, "Thy will be
done on earth as it is in heaven" has the form
of petition, but the substance of it is active
identification of our wishes with God's pur-

poses. Similarly, "Give us this day our daily bread" has the form of asking for a specific, physical thing, but the underlying thought of it is trust, or the recognition of our whole life, in all its details, as having an immediate relation to God's loving plans. This, undoubtedly, is what Jesus meant when he told us that the Father knows what we need before we ask him.

What we need to guard against, however, is being misled by the form of petition into entertaining views of prayer that are inconsistent with this revelation of fatherhood.

*Fourth.* Still another cause of the decreasing assertiveness of prayer, is the habit of scrutinizing more closely the results of prayer. Not many years ago a great deal was heard about "answers" to prayer, and stories of apparent interpositions of supernatural power in response to specific request therefor were industriously circulated. If such accounts are still current to some extent they are less believed than they once were. Rightly or wrongly, the Christian sense of the times refuses to measure prayer by such standards. A nation prays for its president, stricken by an assassin, and hovering between life and death, but when his life is not spared, there is little if any sense of discrepancy between the prayer and the outcome. It seems to be admitted that praying about such matters as the weather has no effect upon the weather at all, and that praying about life and death, health and disease, has no effect upon them except what science recognizes as the influence of the mind upon the body. Now, I think there can be no doubt that this change of attitude has gotten many persons into confusion on the whole subject.

Certain it is, at least, that there is wavering at this point. On the one hand, the assertion is still made that such specific events are controlled through prayer, but, on the other hand, believers draw back from every proposal to test this assertion by the only possible method of settling questions of fact, namely, by observation and induction. As a matter of fact, no such induction has ever been made, and the present temper of Christendom gives no reason to believe that it will ever be made. Yet this making of assertions of fact, which we nevertheless fail or refuse to verify, has the appearance of playing fast and loose with the truth. It tends to discredit prayer among those who are indifferent, and to beget confusion in the minds of devout persons, particularly young Christians.

To escape the force of the difficulty that besets the question of "answers" to prayer, resort is had to two ideas which constitute— unintentionally, of course—evasions. It is said that if what we pray for is not granted, either our faith was not strong enough, or else we asked what is not in accordance with the will of God. The inference would be that we *can* have faith that is strong enough, and that we *can* know whether we are asking in accordance with God's will. But, in fact, this explanation is offered after the prayer fails; it is an effort to break the force of disappointment over what was at the time supposed to meet these conditions. In other words, there is simply no way whereby one can know, when one prays, that these supposed conditions of prevailing prayer are met.

Discussion of this kind is distasteful, as it ought to be, to the spiritual mind. It tends to put prayer on an unspiritual or half-spiritual plane. But, as our first duty is to make an accurate diagnosis, it was necessary to point out the fact that we have only half given up a view of prayer that, in practice, we have largely outgrown. We are rightly impatient with the question of "answers" to prayer, because we have found the reason for prayer in prayer itself. It is a way whereby we experience all things as ours, whether things present or things to come. We need not wait to observe the outcome. Prayer is not merely means to an end, but its end is in itself. It is not a link in a chain of causes, but the realization of eternity above time and change.

*Fifth.* A final disturbing, or at least retarding, factor is the unwise manner in which efforts have been made to build up the prayer life. In the first place, the call to a higher plane of prayer has too often been coupled with a call to retain obsolescent modes of doctrinal belief. In fact, prayer has often been presented as though it were simply unprogressive theology practically applied. In the second place, types of prayer that are determined by temperament have been held up as models for the emulation of all. The credulous man has been exalted above the man of critical intellect, and tears have been habitually preferred to action. The tendency of these two mistakes is to create an impression that the more valuable forms of prayer are reserved for a special class of persons. This impression, too, is unconsciously fostered by the adulation that is bestowed upon men, often young men, who cultivate a particular type of prayer, and talk a great deal about it. What we need more than almost anything else is to cultivate in timid souls that tend to self-distrust, in critical souls that think before they assert, and in active souls that prefer giving to receiving, a robust respect for their own natural types of prayer. At the same time it would not come amiss if the promoters of progressive religious thought should take a little more pains than they commonly do to show how a prayer life of the highest type adjusts itself to the new ideas.

### Our Paradoxical Situation.

These, as I believe, are the causes of our confusion and hesitation. One other apparent cause, however, must be named. The present rapid increase of material prosperity has undoubtedly tended to engross the attention of men with the things of the visible world. By their actions, if not by their words, men are saying that they have gotten riches, and are in

need of nothing, whereas they know not that
they are wretched and miserable and poor and
blind and naked. Jesus' statement of the
difficulty with which a rich man enters into
the kingdom of heaven is as true as it is un-
welcome to those who need it most. And
our age as a whole needs it. For in spite of
all existing social and industrial distress, this
generation is the wealthy one of all history.
This is tenfold true respecting the wealthy
and well-to-do classes which compose the
chief part of the church membership of our
country. Because we are well fed, well
housed, and free from depressing anxiety as
to the physical means of future subsistence, we
tend to lose the sense of dependence. Life
comes to be interpreted in terms of getting
and spending. Possibly large gifts to church
and to philanthropies become an unconscious
substitute for prayer—as though the maintenance of Christian institutions could compen-
sate for the decay of personal communion with
God!

Let us not blink or minimize this tendency
of material prosperity to make us forget.
But let us not stop at this statement of the
fact. Thus far we have touched only the

outside of the question. We must not state
the fact as though Christianity were better
adapted to the hour of pain than to the hour
of rejoicing; or as though it had a message
for poverty that it has not also for plenty; or
as though the Christ were chiefly a compensation for the loss of other things. This
would be the same as admitting Nietsche's
criticism of Christianity, that it is a refuge of
weak natures. If this were so, Christianity,
in performing its task of removing distress,
would remove the chief reason for its own
existence. On the other hand, the impla-
cable insistence with which our religion attacks
all forms of distress, witnesses to its own consciousness that only in and through prosperity
can it come to its highest estate as a power
in the world. If, then, prosperity seems to
unnerve it, we must look for the cause in
something deeper than the mere fact of our
possessing enough things to raise us above
anxiety. We must assume that some side of
Christianity, through which it might demonstrate its power in these new conditions, has
been neglected. Least of all does "worldliness" explain any weakening of the prayer
habit and the prayer spirit. Worldliness is

simply a name for that very fact, and the fact is not accounted for by naming it.

Let us plow deeper, then, than the platitude that prosperity begets worldliness, and worldliness paralyzes the spirit of prayer. The question is, why this happens, and how the tendency to it can be counteracted.   May it not be that one cause is the habitual identification of prayer with asking for things?   If the people believe that prayer is asking for things, then, in proportion as their wants are satisfied, their conscious need of prayer will grow less.   According to this, the person who least needs to pray is the saint who possesses money!   Prayer would then tend to extinguish itself in proportion to its proper and successful exercise.

But another cause of our difficulty, as we have just seen, is the purification of our idea of God, and the spiritualization of the notion of life.   Behold our paradoxical situation: Prayer is one of the most characteristic acts of religion; yet religious progress has involved us in confusion and hesitation regarding it. Prayer is one of the characteristic facts of the life of Jesus; yet the increasing assimilation of his own teaching of the fatherhood of God takes the emphasis out of our own prayers. This paradox must not be dodged, but faced and solved. We are reaping just what we have sown. If the seed is good, so is the crop; and if the crop is partly bad, then bad seed was mixed with the good.

In our efforts to solve this paradox and to reinstate prayer, we must take no step backward toward pre-Christian or non-Christian conceptions of God or of human life. If defective prayer life results from or accompanies truly Christian teaching and aspiration, then we must assume that this teaching and this aspiration have been mixed up with non-Christian elements, which are the real source of our trouble.

The present duty, accordingly, is to take our Christian principles in greater earnest, and develop them to greater clearness.

Thus it comes about that we cannot quite separate our study of the prayer life from our consciousness that two competing types of thought are offering themselves to us as expounders of the religion of Christ. The one defends dogmatic authority in matters of belief, insists upon a philosophy that puts God and the world in sharp antithesis, and in practical religion places the emphasis upon individual salvation. The other type takes a freer attitude toward matters of belief by subordinating them to and testing them by the Christly spirit in the life. By its doctrine of the immanence of God, it brings God and the world together at every point. Further, it accepts love as an adequate index of the character of God, and in harmony therewith calls attention to the social elements in Jesus' conception of salvation. Finally, in practical religion, it places the accent upon the will to do God's will by service of fellowmen.

The former of these two types has too often assumed without evidence that it is a special bulwark of all the subjective states and processes that are summed up under the term "piety," while the latter type has been too tolerant toward this assumption. History does not justify it. Mysticism, which emphasizes the inner, experiential side of religion, has always tended (though not always with success) to burst through the limits of dogmatic Christianity. The mystic, finding within himself a well of water springing up into everlasting life, is less inclined than the dogmatist to drink from the cisterns of tradition; God is to the mystic such a present reality that historical revelations become only a part of a universal self-impartation of God; the delights of mystical communion, moreover, interpret the nature of God in terms of love; and the experienced nearness of God, finally, glorifies the life that now is until there is begotten the universal sympathy that made St. Francis of Assisi call even the animals his brothers. In a broad way, all this is in contrast to ecclesiasticism, dogmatism, and all the mechanical processes of salvation flowing therefrom, while it has an equally marked relationship to the more progressive type of modern theology. Even though modern thought lays more stress upon action than upon contemplation, even though it develops vastly further the social aspects of the Christian life, nevertheless its historical affinity is for mysticism, to which, more than to any other historical movement, we owe what vitality there is in Christian prayer.

It is one of the anomalies of history that the evangelical movement, which has spread among the people the better elements of mysticism, has been so slow to perceive its own theological affinities. In practice, the evan-

gelical movement brings God near to the soul;
yet in theory, it has too often joined itself with
a theology that puts him far away.    Illustrat-
ing this by reference to prayer, we may say
that, though this movement has revived the
life of prayer and of personal communion with
God, it has nevertheless talked of prayer in
the terms of the same dogmatic quasi-deism
that made the evangelical movement a
necessity!

Here we touch the nerve of our present
difficulty; here is our paradox and the solution thereof.    The prayer life suffers to-day,
not more from a failure to bring practice up
to theory, than from a failure to bring theory
up to practice!

*The Way Out and the Way Upward.*

The way out of our paradoxical situation,
and the way upward into a fuller realization
of the possibilities of prayer is, then, not to
call "down brakes!" to the modern tendencies
of Christian thought that seem to disturb the
prayer life, but to add to their momentum if
we can.    First, we must emphasize still more
the idea of service as the true test and measure of piety.    It is not the whole of piety, but

it is the true thermometer of the soul. It is the co-operation with God which is essential to Christian prayer. Second, we must war to the utmost upon the baneful distinction between the sacred and the secular; but we must so war upon it as to make ourselves more deeply and more habitually conscious that we have no life except our life in God. Third, we must be vastly more in earnest with the thought of the fatherhood and providence of God; but we must see that the fatherhood of God can be appropriated by us only through the childlike communion that takes to him everything that concerns us. Fourth, what measure shall we use when we would learn the efficacy of prayer? Shall we search for some extraordinary event which shall astonish the multitude, and puzzle the man of science? Shall we measure prayer, as we measure dollars, by counting and computation? As well might we measure our friendships by tangible benefits received; as well might we value honesty by the extent to which it is shown to be profitable.

It is time, in short, to take two deliberate steps, with a firm determination to abide by the consequences. First, we must sincerely abandon the quasi-deism which Dr. Bowne has happily called "the false supernatural." He says: "In popular thought, religious and irreligious alike, the natural is supposed to be something that runs itself without any internal guidance or external interference. The supernatural, on the other hand, if there be any such thing, is not supposed to manifest itself through the natural, but by means of portents, prodigies, interpositions, departures from, or infractions of, natural law in general. The realm of law belongs to the natural; and the natural runs itself. Hence, if we are to find anything supernatural, we must look for it in the abnormal, the chaotic, the lawless, or that which defies all reduction to order that may be depended on. This notion underlies the traditional debate between naturalism and supernaturalism, and abides in many minds unto this day. . . . . This unhappy misconception of the relation of the natural to the supernatural has practically led the great body of uncritical thinkers into the grotesque inversion of all reason—the more law and order, the less God." (*Zion's Herald*, August 22, 1900.) We fall victims to this fallacy whenever we employ prayer as a means for modifying any of God's regular modes of procedure, whether in nature or in the spiritual life, and also whenever we endeavor to show the efficacy of prayer by exhibiting any apparent departure from this regular procedure. We must look upon natural law as simply God's way of doing things, and invariable because his intelligence and his purpose change not. The one God must not be split up into a God of nature *plus* a God who answers prayer, but nature itself must be looked upon as a part of the one divine process that has been called the moral order.

A second necessary step is the re-working of our conception of prayer into terms of personal relationship, pure and simple. The unspiritual view of prayer includes three factors—the praying soul, God, and a third something desired by the soul and obtainable only through God. A fitting symbol thereof would be a triangle of such a sort as to permit motion along its sides in only one direction. The soul is at one corner, the desired object is at another, but the soul can reach this object only by going around two sides of the triangle ; that is, through God, who is at the third corner. We think of prayer

as a means of getting something for ourselves or for another, and it is only when
things turn out according to our wishes that
we exclaim that they must be "providential."
What we must do is to make God end and
not means.    The symbol that fits prayer is
not a triangle, for there are not three factors
in the conception, but only two, God and his
child.    Even a line, with God at one end and
man at the other, may not serve as a symbol
of it, for prayer, in its higher forms, aims to
be an actual meeting of God and the soul.
At its highest, it is the conscious realization,
in some degree, of the union with God that
is the supreme end of living.

If this be mysticism, it is the heart thereof
and not its excrescences.    We do not approve
mysticism as a whole, with all its excesses and
all its misunderstood psychology, when we say
that in spite of these it contains the sound
kernel of Christianity and of all religion.    The
Christian conception of God is couched in
terms of a personal relationship on his part
toward men.    The Christian conception of
life is defined in terms of personal relationship
to God and to our fellows.    Now, this personal relation between us and our Father, in

order to be complete, must include the possibility that, through mutual sympathy between God and his child, through a mutual giving of self, the one to the other, each shall feel himself living not merely in himself, but in the other also. This is prayer in the most complete sense of the term. It is not a mere indulgence in religious emotion, or a selfish appropriation of divine benefits, since such sympathy, such union, as this includes the adoption of God's will as our own, and active consecration thereto.

Prayer, then, carries its end, its justification, its efficacy in itself. It needs no other reason for existing than just what it is in itself. Yet this does not imply that the efficacy of prayer ends here. For surely the man who joins himself with God does not leave the universe just what it was before. All things are bound together into unity. I drop a pebble from my hand; it falls to earth, but the great earth rises to meet it. They seek a common center of gravity, determined by the mass of one as truly as by that of the other. You cannot change any one thing without changing something else also. The man who prays changes the center of gravity of the world of persons. Other persons will be different as well as himself, and he could not have produced this difference by any other means than this union of himself with God.

It has been suggested that, by a subtle sensitiveness of soul for soul, such as the term "telepathy" is intended to describe, the man who prays may perform a specific vicarious act for another. Intercession would then become a phase of telepathy, and would take its place under the general notion of psychological law. This is not the place for discussing the tenability of such an hypothesis. Yet a warning must be uttered. No such speculation as this should be made into a support, or apparent support, of prayer, nor should apparent answers to prayer be too readily adduced in support of the hypothesis. Hypotheses concerning the laws of the mind must be judged by scientific method, and that alone. At present, the hypothesis of telepathy is so far from commanding the general assent of scientific men that we should only discredit prayer if we should make it appear that there is any vital connection between the two.

Having given a rather mystical turn to our

discussion, I must now hasten to say that what has been described is not all prayer, but only ideal prayer. The ideal, however, gives its own character to every effort to realize it, and so there are many kinds and degrees of true prayer. We cannot deny this name to any effort, however feeble, however confused, to come into personal relations with God. Not only conscious union with him, but also every sincere step toward such union, is prayer.

Again, prayer varies in its constituents according to age, temperament, and circumstances. A child cannot commune with God precisely as one who has experienced the realities of mature life, nor should youthful Christians be tempted to imitate the prayer life of older persons. There is danger, in fact, whenever one person undertakes to mold his praying on the figure of another. Differences of temperament, training, and circumstance are so great that misunderstandings and disappointments arise. To one, prayer is chiefly emotional fellowship; to another, it is more largely self-devotion to Godlike moral ideals; to a third, it expresses the impulse to action; to a fourth, it is reverent reflectiveness in the presence of the deepest truths of life and destiny.   It would be worth while to be all these persons at once, but until we become far more symmetrical than we are now, we should avoid setting up any one of ourselves as a standard.   The one demand upon us all is that we should strive, each in the way that expresses his own soul, to establish ideal personal relations with God.   This, whatever form it takes, is prayer.

A little child, seeing a storm cloud rising, stops his play, kneels on the lawn, and begs God not to let it rain.   This is real prayer; not because the child requests a particular favor, but because he assumes toward God a personal relation that is appropriate for a little child.   He makes the entirely Christian assumption that the All-Father is interested in even the games of childhood.

Just so, the simple believer who asks that he may have rain for his wheat-field, truly prays.   His praying will not alter the order of nature, in which rain has its place, but through his prayer he assumes a relation of conscious dependence and trust toward God, and rightly assumes that God is interested in wheat.   By bringing his daily occupation to God, the farmer attains to something greater than wheat, however—to a spiritual relationship that is of ultimate worth.

Another, forgetful of things about him, asks that his own life and character may become better. The response that God makes will not include any departure from the universal laws of spiritual growth, for character is not bestowed, it must be acquired through obedience. Nevertheless, this is a high order of prayer, because it strives to establish personal relations with God on the plane of his moral purposes.

For the same reason, there is true prayer in every feeling, thought, and act, by which we make God's point of view our own. There is prayer in all intentional co-operation with the divine purpose. Thus, reflection upon truth may be prayer, as Augustine taught us to see; and also the doing of homely duties, as Brother Lawrence showed us in his kitchen. For every age of life, for every temperament, for every occupation, for every circumstance, the one essential is effort toward personal relations of sympathy and co-operation with God.

We might express this idea briefly by calling prayer *social life between man and God*.

What effect will this view have upon our special times for prayer? If, as we have seen, the ideal life of prayer is a life in which every thought, every emotion, every act of our own is at the same time a social relationship between us and God, then the only complete prayer is the Christian life in its totality. When our lives reach this plane, special seasons of prayer will be superfluous, and in proportion as we approach it, we should expect special times and places to have less and less significance for us.

But let us not deceive ourselves. We have just been talking about ideal manhood, not about this actual life of fragments and of imperfections. Let us not fail to keep the ideal before us, but at the same time let us be practical.

A mother and a father, through labor and sacrifice, bring up a son, educate him, and send him forth from home to fulfil some mission that is dear to them as it is also to him. In his daily labor the son is really co-operating with his parents. He thinks their thoughts, feels with them, makes their purposes his own. Yet, ever and anon, the impulse seizes him to visit the old homestead, that he may talk with them face to face. Somewhat so, though our heavenly Father is never absent from us, yet our attention is too untrained, too narrow, to be always conscious of him. We forget him in various degrees, from positive sin to the unspiritual assumption that the things with which our occupation has to do are secular rather than sacred. And so, just because we are what we are, we need special times in which to recall our thoughts from all that is false, from all that is artificial, from all that is less than God. We need to talk to our Father, face to face.

# THE CONSCIOUSNESS OF SIN

# CHAPTER XII

## THE CONSCIOUSNESS OF SIN

From the days of Paul until now the Christian conception of life has been to a remarkable extent dominated by the thought of deliverance from sin. The fall of man and his bondage to evil have been looked upon as the ultimate reason for the whole Christian scheme. The life and death of Christ, the whole history of the chosen people which preceded, and the whole spread of the kingdom of God which followed, have been conceived as a remedial process, a method of restoring what had been lost. Under this view, the destiny of each man is simply escape or failure to escape from sin and its consequences. Here has been found the motive and the method of the Christian propaganda in both heathen and Christian lands. The basis of Christian experience has been found in a previous experience of alienation; and personal religious culture, even the religious nurture of children, has been controlled by the all-pervading thought of sin.

*Prominence of the Idea of Sin in Christian
    Life and Theology.*

If release from the harsher phases of this
conception has already been won, and if
advancing thought has secured a larger horizon, it remains true, nevertheless, that sin is
still the controlling conception of very much
of the popular thought of our religion.    It is
not too late to ask, Why should this be so?
Certainly the religious instinct of mankind at
large, as shown in the history of religion,
gives to the sense of sin no such place as this.
Religion does not arise through consciousness
of guilt, nor is this the chief factor in the religious development of the world; nor did the
teachings of Jesus give it this place of prominence.    Not only was he silent concerning all
the vast conception of a fallen race which
forms the *raison d'être* of the "plan of salvation," but his direct practical teachings are
not largely aimed at rescuing men from a consciousness of guilt.    There is infinite sympathy with the sick, the sorrowing, the
heavy laden, but no similar manifestation of
feeling toward the tortures of a guilty conscience.    There is, of course, the sharpest

distinction between false and true living, but always with a view to making true life attractive and commanding. With the possible exception of his denunciation of the Pharisees, it does not appear, either, that Jesus made any effort to induce a feeling of being guilty and lost.

With Paul, however, we find a rich development of the idea of sin—its entrance into the world, the ruin wrought by it, the sense of alienation and despair, the need of reconciliation, the work of Christ as deliverer and reconciler. This is not the place for undertaking to account for this phase of Paul's thinking, except in a rough, general way. It is sufficient to note that his training as a Pharisee, his personal experience, the natural reaction of a temperament like his in contact with the sins of the ancient world, would tend to produce a specially keen appreciation of divine law, transgression, condemnation, and justification.

That the same attitude should be characteristic of theology for many generations was no less natural. For the contrast between the pure teachings and life of Jesus and the moral decay of the Roman world, together

with the persecutions which the religion of
love endured, could not but create a sense of
intense contrast between sin and righteousness, a deep realization of the world's sinfulness, and vivid insight into the need of Christ
because of sin. Add to this that the omnipresent, organizing genius of Rome begot a
habit of thinking personal relations under legal
and judicial forms, and it will not appear
strange that Christian thought consolidated so
firmly about the notion of sin and violated
law.

Further strength was given to this way of
thinking by the struggle of Christianity with
other forms of heathenism than the Roman.
The conversion of Teutonic tribes, for example, could not at once root out the Teutonic
mythology. In the thinking of the converted
tribes, their former gods became devils. The
old beliefs were not washed away by baptism,
but merely transformed into an orthodox
demonology. Witchcraft was the result. In
its highest development, the witchcraft belief
is a complete system of doctrine concerning
Satan and evil spirits corresponding almost
point for point with the doctrine of God and the
good spirits who are his messengers. Over

against the kingdom of God was the kingdom of Satan, and these two, in their struggle for the mastery, were so nearly matched that each was obliged to employ strategy and deception as well as force when hard pressed. The battle-field of these two world-powers was the mind of man. In every human breast God and Satan were soliciting allegiance, and our most familiar friend, whose life seemed pure and high-minded, might actually be under contract to serve the enemy of God.

So firmly did this general conception fix itself in Christian thought, that a post-reformation theologian, a Protestant, declared that two things are essential to salvation, to know the true God, and to know the true devil. If, since that time, we have come to look upon creation as God's world, not the devil's, not a divided kingdom, the gain has not been made without protest, and the good work is not yet done. Belief in a personal devil has been insisted upon as an essential item of orthodox doctrine, and an intimate sense of Satan's presence in moments of temptation has added brilliancy to what has passed for Christian experience. The soul is still looked upon as a battle-field of contending desires.

Though Satan and his angels but rarely appear to the eyes of modern saints as they did to those of other days, yet popular conceptions of the Christian life still focus around the notion of sin. Even the churches have not recovered from the effects of this conception upon the training of children. We no longer say, or distinctly believe, that children are lost or must become lost before they belong to the kingdom of God, nor do we strive, as the fathers did, to awaken in them fears and anguish. But, for all that, we permit children to think that coming to God is identical with escaping from sin and guilt, and by our neglect of positive nurture we encourage them to count themselves as outside the fold until they are rescued from a life of sin.

A further consequence of this emphasis upon sin is, that many young persons hesitate to become disciples because they fear that they cannot live up to a certain standard of holiness. Young Christians frequently doubt their religious standing because they fall into faults which they hate. Growth in grace is measured by the decreasing power of positive sin, and fitness for the judgment is estimated by the degree of holiness, or absence of sinful stains.   Similarly, the cultivation of what is variously called the higher life, holiness, and entire sanctification has been based upon the notion of sin and sinfulness.   The aim has been release, rest of soul, and the process has been looked upon as a cleansing of the soul from original sin, or from all inward inclination to evil.

Revivals of religion, at least those of the typical form, have had sin as their central *motif*.   A process practically as fixed as that of a factory has been set going.   The sinner has, first of all, been worked upon with a view to a deep conviction of sin, a deep feeling of his lost and helpless condition.   When this has been secured, and not till then, the revivalist has felt that the way is open for a "sound conversion."   Then God's pardoning grace has been offered, and finally, after conversion is supposed to have occurred, the convert is sometimes offered a positive task to perform for the Master.

## Present Decay of the Consciousness of Sin.

Much of this description applies, in strictness, rather to the generation just passing away than to the younger generation.   The sense of sin is certainly not present as it once was. Few sermons are heard in these days on "the exceeding sinfulness of sin," "the lost and ruined state of the natural man," "the wrath of God," and the "awfulness of the day of judgment." Comparatively few church members of the younger generation have ever passed through any distinct realization of the "terrors of the law." They have come into church fellowship by some smoother, less tragic process. A contemporary psychologist, remarking upon the fact that the progress of evolution from brute to man involves a great decrease in the occasions for fear, says: "In civilized life, in particular, it has at last become possible for large numbers of people to pass from the cradle to the grave without ever having had a pang of genuine fear." (James: "Psychology, Briefer Course," New York, 1892, p. 408.) With slight modifications, this proposition would describe the movement of religion as well as that of civilization in general. There is far less fear, less notion of escaping, less consciousness of a *vis a tergo*.

This change is frequently noticed and deplored. For many persons believe that the old way is the better.  They complain that admission to the church has been made too easy; that, not insisting upon deep conviction for sin, we have filled our rolls with the names of unconverted or half-converted persons; that this decrease of emphasis upon sin is the source of many a fault in church life, of many a weakness of the church in its relations to the world, and that the way to recover power is to preach the wrath of God.

However much or little wisdom there may be in this reactionary demand, the situation certainly calls for a re-examination of the proper function of the sense of sin.  Is sin the fact from which Christianity derives its significance?  Are repulsion toward sin and desire to escape its consequences the central motive for coming to Christ, and for living the Christ-life?  We have here a question that goes to the bottom of Christian experience, and doubtless, of theology also.  Let us consider it from the standpoint of experience only.

First, let us ask why the sense of sin has undergone a decline in the recent history of the Christian church?  When we have answered this question, we shall be ready to ask whether or not this movement is in the general direction of progress, and this inquiry will lead us back, finally, to Jesus, whose mind, at this point, we shall try to interpret.

Why has the sense of sin become a less prominent factor of the Christian consciousness? First, because of all the influences that have tended to produce a general readjustment of attitude with respect to the relations of doctrine and life. We have less and less inclination to assume that a doctrine that is not based upon experience must be verified by or transformed into experience. We cannot longer allow that the doctrine is a fixed standard to which life must adjust itself, but we insist, rather, that life is primary, and that theory must be derived therefrom. This is implied in the whole movement of the modern intellect. Now, the old-fashioned experience of the sense of sin was largely a factitious product of the ruling theory of sin. The ruin wrought by Adam's transgression, the sinfulness of our nature, the immeasurable distance of such a nature from God and heaven—all this, firmly believed and constantly preached by earnest, sincere men, was well fitted to work upon the emotions through the imagination, and to produce the precise sense of being lost that the theory called for. But this was an artificial process. It was experiencing a doctrine. At its best, it furnished a partial and misleading expression for the actual conflict with concrete evil; at its worst, it became scarcely distinguishable from an emotional drama.

That such preaching had this better side is clear. It brought many a man to a realization of his actual transgressions. Wilful, neglectful, self-indulgent violators of their own conscience were often brought to a halt, and to this extent the work was not factitious. But the preaching of the law did not stop here. It went on to impose the same terrors upon all persons alike, even little children. Those whom Jesus set before us as an illustration of the kingdom of God were impelled to penitence. As we have seen, the first aim of catechetical instruction was to convince the catechumen of his lost condition, to the end that he might become sorry for his sins, or rather for his relation to Adam's transgression.

We need not undervalue this preaching of sin in order to be convinced that its artificial element was doomed to lose influence in mod-

ern life.  We need not even deny the doctrine
in order to see that Christian experience ought
to be more natural, more real, more closely
related to the personal conscience.  "We're
sunk enough here, God knows;" we need no
artificial incitements to repentance; and what
is more, the thirst for reality which marks the
modern mind condemns such incitements.

A second reason for the decline of the
sense of sin is, that the "terrors of the law"
appealed to motives not high enough to move
the modern conscience profoundly.  The
"personal salvation" which men were ex-
horted to seek is a purely individualistic good.
Of course, self-regarding motives have an
abiding place in religion.  But when the great
business of life is understood to be the securing of one's own salvation, then self-regarding
motives are made supreme, and one's religion
is tainted with immorality.  No doubt the
preaching of Christ, even in perverted modes,
leads men toward good works, and tends to
purify the motives for them.  Christ overrules
his ambassadors.  Yet we must not close our
eyes to the fact that good deeds, which to the
modern conscience have their end in themselves, were looked upon as mere corollaries

of salvation, or conditions of retaining it. They became part of a process whose end lies beyond itself.    This was the atmosphere of the whole Christian life.    Why should I do this, or refrain from that? was answered by exhibiting its relationship to a scheme of salvation which terminates in the mind of God or in the bliss of heaven.

Naturally enough, this self-regarding view of life never could wholly dominate life.    The constitution of the moral nature is against it. The sweet influences of Jesus' life and words worked in and through imperfect notions so that men builded better than they knew.    And when, as in modern life, presuppositions come to the test, any such theory of life as that just described becomes ineffective.

This brings us to a third reason why the sense of sin has grown comparatively weak, namely, the modern tendency to emphasize positive good in every sphere of life.    There was a time when the race had to struggle for existence against nature.    But that time is long past. Wild beasts have been conquered; the rigors of the seasons have been provided against; effective methods have been found for obtaining and distributing food; the ravages of disease have been checked by preventive measures—in short, we have little occasion to defend ourselves against nature, but only to exploit natural resources for our own benefit. In particular, as was shown in an earlier chapter, modern science and invention have tended to induce a sense of our mastery of nature. We are at last able to look cheerfully ahead, to be led from before instead of being driven from behind. Life has come to mean something very positive, and we measure it, not by what it escapes of evil, but by what it contains of blessing.

Religion shares in this movement of the human spirit. The older fashion was to concentrate attention upon legal righteousness. The highest blessedness was, so to speak "a clean slate." This accorded with the spirit of Jewish and Roman law; it fitted the formalistic temper of the mediæval mind; it harmonized with the sense of struggling against nature for life and the means thereto. But the movement of the modern mind has been away from mere logical consistency, mere legal rectitude, mere escape from anything, and toward the securing of rich content for thought, and a positive filling for life. Aspiration reaches out beyond innocence, beyond acquittal, beyond acceptance with God; we dare to insist that life and religion shall find their justification in that toward which they tend.

The shifting of interest from the evils that are to be feared to the good that is to be worked for is a remarkable fact. It has helped to reform instruction and discipline throughout systems of education. It has humanized the administration of prisons and of institutions for the defective and delinquent classes. It has begun to reform judicial procedure and legislation. It is working as a yeast through the whole industrial system. Most remarkable of all is its influence upon the tone of popular consciousness. The common people have acquired a habit of looking up as well as behind and about. There is in the atmosphere an invigorating sense of ends that are worth striving for. The positive, the concrete, the something that is to be had or done or enjoyed is what appeals to the popular mind.

Applied to the daily life of the Christian, this movement leads one to give little attention to status, but much to accomplishment;

little to defects, but much to duties. The Christian consciousness is moving toward a point where the supreme question of life will be not, "Am I saved?" but "What am I good for?" Not, "Does God pardon and accept me?" but "How can I contribute most to the progress of the kingdom of God?" Day by day, when the Christian reaches the reflective hour at the close of daily work, he will ask not, "What sin have I committed this day?" but "What can I learn from this day that will make me more efficient to-morrow?"

## *Does the Decreased Sense of Sin Indicate a General Decline of Religion?*

There may be other causes for the decay of the sense of sin, but they will hardly be found as effective as these three. Possibly some persons will question whether the most important cause of all has not been omitted. They will ask whether the loss of the consciousness of sin is not, in fact, simply an increasing fondness for sin, due to increasing indulgence therein. This might conceivably be the case. Sin, persistently indulged in, blunts the moral perceptions until one's judgment of one's self becomes a mere mechanical

approval of what one is.   But surely the
Christian world of to-day is not characterized
by blunted moral perception.   The Christian
consciousness is puzzled, to be sure, by some
things that it has to face for the first time,
and it therefore manifests some hesitation.   It
may temporarily slacken its speed in order
that it may turn a corner to which its own
progress has brought it.   It has shortcomings
which it needs to repair.   But it shows, in
general, no sign of the seared conscience.

On the contrary, the Christian consciousness of to-day includes a marked revival of
the sense of responsibility.   To take a most
obvious example, the day of pious, self-satisfied alms-giving is gone, and we stand consciously facing the far more solemn duty of
removing the causes of human misery.   Poverty used to be taken for granted, as though it
were a heaven-ordained opportunity for exer-
cising the virtue of compassionate giving;
but to-day the existence of poverty is a re-
buke to the conscience.   We realize that we
are, to some extent, responsible for its existence.   As this realization grows, a lower form
of conscientiousness gives place to a higher.

The change at this point is thoroughly

characteristic of the new Christian consciousness. What we are doing is to question the
presuppositions of older forms of goodness,
and the result, in perhaps every case, is an
increase of moral strenuousness. Take the
Christian view of wealth as a further example.
It has passed through many stages. Men
now living can remember when "giving to the
Lord" a small fraction of one's income was
the accepted mark of the consecration of a
man of wealth. To-day more searching questions are asked. Conscience "goes behind
the returns." It asks, "How am I acquiring
property? Am I receiving more than my just
share of the joint products of labor and capital? Do I love my employees as myself?
Am I cheerfully paying my whole share of the
public taxes? Further, why should *I* possess
wealth, anyhow? Wealth is not end, but
means. To what end is my wealth being
made a means? How is the world better off
because I have power?" Thus the kingdom
of God presses itself home to the modern
conscience as the only real end of living. It
refuses to compromise or divide benefits; it
makes its own presuppositions, not accommo-
dating itself to conditions, but molding condi-

tions themselves.   It demands the whole of a man's being and of his possessions.

This quickened conscience is not confined to a few who preach to the many, nor is it a mere dreamy sentiment.   It is present in Christianity as an active ferment.   Its demands, to be sure, have only begun to be felt and to be acted upon.   The church is, in fact, staggering under the discovery of how much it means to be Christian.   Yet already the heavenly vision is beginning to secure obedience.   Its signs are everywhere.   They can be read in church work for the city masses; in missionary enterprise; in philanthropic institutions; in efforts to give the children of the cities a chance for a good life; in the statutory amelioration of industrial conditions; in the whole social movement; and in the movement of giving which is fast bringing into public discredit the notion that a man may get all he can and do with it what he pleases.

A parallel quickening of conscience may be observed through the whole range of religious interests.   The religious motive is coming closer to life as a whole.   It is organizing itself as never before.   We begin to look upon the conversion of the heathen world as a "business proposition," which we must attend to with the same wide and wise planning as that which is given to commerce and manufacturing. The work of missions is not to be a specialty of the very pious, but the everyday duty of all Christians. We are coming to see, in short, that it is our "business" to take Christ to all men, and if such phenomena as the student volunteer movement mean anything, we shall soon see a new type of organized and well-supported work in the foreign fields.

Another striking example of the robustness as well as sensitiveness of the present-day conscience is found in the new realization of the significance of religion for the whole man. Jesus went about healing bodies, but many of his disciples have fancied that the exclusive mission of the church is to save souls. To-day we are moving back toward Christ through the discovery that our religion can touch men, and ought to do so, through the whole range of their nature—physical, mental, and moral. The gymnasiums and evening classes of the Young Men's Christian Associations, the social clubs of the college settlements, and

the varied activities of institutional churches testify to a genuine awakening of the Christian conscience.

Examples like these could easily be multiplied. They show that not only is the lessened sense of sin not to be interpreted as a hardening of conscience, but on the contrary they suggest the question whether this remarkable coincidence between a decline in the sense of sin and a growth in the sense of Christian duty is not itself significant of an essential relation between the two. Is it not possible that, as our sense of the positive content of the Christian life grows, it crowds out the sense of those negative impulsions that gather about the thought of actual or possible guilt? Instead of being a retrograde movement, then, is not the declining consciousness of sin the displacement of a lower by a higher type of Christian experience?

Several considerations, in addition to those already given, may be adduced in support of this hypothesis. In the first place, there is a distinct gain in sincerity, in reality, in the moralizing of life when we abandon the effort to induce an experience of sin through the dogma of the fall, or, indeed, through any

teaching other than that of our own experience of life. Being "saved" comes to mean more. Instead of being a judicial fact or decision it becomes just the Christlike life itself. This brings religion close home to us. There is less chance for substituting something else for the practical things that the Lord, our God, requires of us.

Again, a little consideration of the psychology of the moral life will show that a positive aspiration has a force for good which a negative impulsion cannot possess. Under the law of suggestion we tend to become like our habitual thought of ourselves. One's health can be affected for good or for ill by one's thought of it. Similarly, the power of evil lies, in large measure, in the tendency of idea to pass into act irrespective of our deliberation. Resistance to evil should begin by banishing the thought of it. But how can ideas be banished from the mind? Only by turning the attention to other ideas. Hence it follows that we can attain our highest possibilities only by habitual thinking upon the things that are lovely and of good report.

This is a mere rudiment of moral hygiene, but just because it is a rudiment, its impor-

tance is inexpressibly great. Doubtless many a man has become fixed in sin chiefly through reflecting that sins like his are natural to humankind. How can a youth be more surely corrupted than by placing him in a social atmosphere which, without justifying this or that sin, nevertheless always thinks of it as a product of our constitution? If, when you try to cross a stream upon a single plank, you fix your eyes upon the water beneath, you invite disaster. If, when you wish to sleep, you entertain the fear of staying awake, you take the straight road toward insomnia. Habitually associate the notion of sin with the thought of what you are, and you will gravitate in that direction. This is true, even though you hate the sin which you contemplate. Watch it intently, and it will fascinate you as the serpent's glittering eye charms a song-bird.

Considering these things, one may be pardoned for doubting whether the sense of sin ever did work the great good that has been attributed to it. Have not the positive results of the Christian propaganda been reached everywhere and always by exhibiting the positive content of the Christian life rather than

by fixing attention upon sin? It is life that generates life. When the Christ is held before our eyes, he kindles some spark of affection, and what has been called "the expulsive power of a new affection" drives out the evil thing that we once loved. We are saved by hope, not by fear. Our minds are not first emptied of evil and afterward filled with the good, but the emptying and the filling are all one event. Jesus brings life to light. He puts before us something worth living for, and gives us the courage to live for it. In his presence we see what it is to live, and suddenly or gradually we find ourselves daring to hope, to aspire, to choose the highest. The Light which is also the Life of men leads us on. Our attention becomes permanently shifted from all lesser good. Our souls become filled with the thought of the Father and of the Elder Brother, and of their loving attitude toward us. Just here lies the psychology of the influence of Jesus. He moves us by no mechanical process, by no pushing, but by a drawing which consists in filling the mind with positive content of ultimate, commanding worth.

*The Method of the Master.*

Not only, then, are we justified in saying that the present-day quickening of the Christian conscience and the coincident lessening of the sense of sin are one movement of the Christian consciousness, but we may also assert that this is a movement back to the Christ. At the outset of our discussion we noticed what a small place the notion of guilt and of sinfulness has in the teachings of the Master. Now we are ready to ask whether this fact does not show the depth of his spiritual insight, his grasp upon the powers that mold personality.

Under this conception of the positive method of his work he is not less a Saviour than under the notion which dates everything human from the fall of man; but his work is now seen to be remedial because it is creative, because it brings into human life an access of life. It is to be regretted that the mission of Christ has been so largely expressed in figures of speech derived from the practice of medicine. For, however appropriate such figures might be made by careful analysis of the ideas involved, the popular notion of medical practice has made them misleading. The multitude seeks healing through mere medication. No sooner does a disorder appear than inquiry is made as to what shall be "taken" for it. But every wise physician knows that the place now occupied in popular thought and practice by drugging should be taken by hygiene. How shall we protect, increase, and economically apply the energy of the organism? This is the important question. Just so, the central problem of religion is that of moral energy. Jesus' work for us and in us has to do with the vital dynamics of our moral being. He feeds, gives light, guides into channels of wholesome activity—in short, gives us life, and that abundantly. He is the physician of the soul because he teaches the soul how to live, and gives the impulse to follow the teaching.

But, though all this is true, it is only one side of the truth. For Jesus was as far as possible from slurring the fact of sin. His eyes were wide open to the badness as well as the goodness of men. Though his gospel is full of hope and cheer and abundant life, nevertheless he knew nothing of the comfortable, arm-chair optimism that lets the world take its course in the lazy belief that everything is bound to come out right somehow. Indeed, one of the surprising things about Jesus is, that though he placed so little stress upon guilt and upon sinfulness as a condition, he also searched the depths of the conscience, placing concrete good and concrete evil in the sharpest opposition. Nothing in the history of morals cuts so sharply between good and evil as his words and his example. How the Sermon on the Mount, the description of the judgment, the double law of love, pierce through all our armor of self-conceit, self-indulgence, and indifference! With what precision do they classify us and our deeds! And, at the same time that they beautify all the graces of character, they paint concrete sins in the ugliest colors.

There is a sense in which the Christian law of love is the severest moral principle that any teacher has ever imposed upon his disciples. It is severe because of its comprehensiveness, and also because it goes directly to the springs of life. We can obey almost any legalistic scheme more easily than this. The most punctilious Pharisee sets a lighter task before himself than does the man who merely sets out to be kindly to his fellows. It is easier to bestow our goods to feed the poor, yes, to give our bodies to be burned, than it is to make the interests of other men our own. The full capacity of human nature at its highest will not more than barely suffice to fulfil this law. And yet—O Teacher of Paradoxes!—we are told that this yoke is easy, and this burden light! Thus the Christ searches us out, and finds all our sins, and yet ever points us away from the sin to the privilege that lies ahead.

How shall we picture to ourselves Jesus' thought of our relation to sin and guilt? Certainly life is not, in his view, a mere escape from evil, nor does attainment consist in securing acquittal from any court. His message is, that God is not an avenging deity; that he does not hold grudges; that he is not a judge over us, but our Father. We have no occasion to go about to secure pardon. The Father takes the initiative, and seeks to reconcile us, not to condemn us. He is already reconciled to all men of good will, and what he demands of us is, that we put ourselves in this class.

Nor does Jesus picture life as a mere probation, a testing that is preliminary to life indeed. Rather, we are to have life, and have it abundantly here and now. We are, therefore, not waging a defensive fight against the powers of evil, but rather an aggressive fight for the good. The Christian life is, in every sense, an overcoming of evil with good. If we wish a single word for this attitude, we may call it militant; or, better, we may pass from the figure of war to that of industry by calling the Christian attitude that of the worker. To desire to bring something really worth while to pass—this is the Christian attitude toward life as a whole, and this implies all that is included in the Christian attitude toward sin.

We must not, therefore, close our eyes to the evil that is in the world and in ourselves. That would not be the part of a soldier or of a worker. We are commissioned to conquer self, and to make prisoners of the world for Christ. As workers, our orders are to build into our own life and into the life of the community imperishable materials. We have, then, to discriminate, and to recognize the perishable, the sinful, wherever it really exists, and to bring its power to naught. But

there is no duty to entertain a regret that is
not also a motion toward the positive ends of
the kingdom of God. There is no virtue in
thinking upon sin, or in emotional experience
with respect to it, except as these are merely
reverse aspects of aggressive fighting, or of
industrious work upon the eternal temple.

### The Need of a Deepened, but Transformed, Sense of Sin.

At last we are ready to see just where
danger does lie in the present loss of the
sense of sin. It lies in the tendency to a
false optimism, which begins by indulging self
because one has ceased to be afraid, and then
goes on to be indifferent to the needs of the
world. It is the danger of failing to realize
what we are here for, or that we are, in fact,
here for anything beyond our own comfort.
If moral laziness were to be the effect of release from a factitious sense of sin, better the
old-fashioned preaching that shook lazy men
over the flames of the pit until craven fear
moved them to consider the meaning of life.
Such preaching, with all its grotesque hor-
rors, did, at least, administer some moral
tonic. We cannot go back to it, of course,

nor need we fear that we are in the midst of
a decline of the Christian conscience. But
we can be better than we are, and probably
our chief danger is self-indulgent enjoyment
of the sense of security. We have outgrown
certain negative impulses, but positive
Christian principle is not yet full grown within
us. We are learning to forget the things that
are behind, but we do not reach out with
sufficient eagerness for the things that are
before. Realizing that God is in his world,
we must go on to see that God works in the
moral world through us his moral creatures.
We are good only as far as we are good for
something. We need not be anxious about
any personal escape merely as personal, but
we must realize that, just in proportion as we
fail to take our full part in the work of God
in the world, we are lost and alienated from
God, whatever our church affiliations, whatever our beliefs, whatever our religious experiences.

But must not purely negative impulsions
be relied upon for bringing sinners to Christ?
Must we not drive, as well as lead? There
are several directions in which an answer to
this question might be sought. We might

call attention to the preaching of Jesus, which made the idea of the kingdom of God the reason and motive for repentance. We might bring to witness the Christian experience of to-day, which shows that positive incitements actually do bring men to Christ. We might, finally, question our right to divide men into two mutually exclusive classes, the saved and the unsaved, each of which is reached by motives peculiar to itself. The Christ presents but one kind of motive to all men, whatever their condition, and the character of that motive is determined by the divine love, with its positive ends.   There is but one commanding end of life; there is but one humanity to be commanded by it.   We are saved in proportion to our obedience, and not in any higher degree.   The reasons and motives for being more Christian than we are, are the same as those for being Christian at all.

This implies heightening, not lowering, the contrast between good and evil in the Christian consciousness, and it implies no softening of it when we preach Christ to the sinner.   Men are moved, whether they are Christians or not, by the presentation of contrasts.    If we have common sense we will not think that we can move men to accept Christ by soothing their consciences, but only by rousing them to a vivid realization of the great gulf fixed between right and wrong. The real question, then, is not whether we should strive to awaken a sense of sin, but rather in what the sense of sin should consist. Looking to the preaching of Jesus for an answer to this question, we conclude that the sense of sin which we should aim to awaken is a vivid realization of the kingdom of God as a concrete fact set over against the concrete facts of self-love in all its forms.    The awfulness of sin is revealed, not by any abstract, juridical notions, but by actual observation of life.    The use of talents, the spending of our means, the hunger and nakedness about us, the sick and the prisoners, the little children—turn upon these and our relations to them the strong light of the kingdom of God, and no man's conscience can escape conviction.

Several specific influences are tending to produce a thoughtless optimism that favors moral inertia.    The theory of evolution has been falsely interpreted as a doctrine of universal progress. The universe at large appears to contain a secret spring that pushes life upward and ever upward. The inference has been made that therefore the world will take care of itself. There results a sort of *laissez-faire* morality, which tolerates evil rather than take the trouble to fight it. In truth, however, the theory of evolution, as applied to man, recognizes human endeavor as the essential condition of further progress. Rightly understood, the position of man in the evolutionary scheme adds immeasurable solemnity to life. For, when the story of the genesis of things, the story

> " Of tendency through endless ages,
> Of star-dust and star-pilgrimages,
> Of rounded worlds, of space and time,
> Of the old flood's subsiding slime,
> Of chemic matter, force, and form,
> Of poles and powers, cold, wet, and warm,"—

when this story reaches man, we behold our own moral struggle entering into the cosmic process to complete and glorify it. It is as if the whole creation had groaned and travailed in pain waiting for the sense of personal responsibility to be born.

The material prosperity in the midst of which we are living adds to the temptation to a false ease.   In the traditional view of the world, one who has acquired honorable wealth is entitled to the enjoyment of it.  The Christian conscience has begun to see how un-Christian this traditional view is, but it has only begun.   How easily we take for granted that the possession of large means will manifest itself, even in the disciples of Jesus, in luxury and display, and how forgetful we are of the kingdom of God in our efforts to keep "in the swim" of a conventional social life that gauges itself by its expensiveness!   Too much importance is given to things, and too little to personality.   We lazily conform where we ought to raise a higher standard.   In a word, we have much to acquire of the militant, aggressive, business-like attitude and habit.

Jesus came not to send peace, but a sword. He would have us realize, with something of his own keen sympathy, the condition of the world about us.   How much of God's work remains undone right where we live!   A catalogue of the world's sins is not needed to convince us that "the world," as opposed to the kingdom of God, is an awful reality.   It is not sin in the abstract, or personal sinfulness, with which we have chiefly to do, but evil in the concrete, the bad life and the suffering life that we may make better and happier.

How shall we measure our responsibility for this concrete sin? Not alone by asking what specific wrong acts we contribute to it, but also by asking what we might do to mitigate it. What the Christian world needs is a new sense of guilt, a realization on the part of each of us that I am taking part in the sin of the world, that I am responsible for its misery to the extent to which I might prevent the one and relieve the other. Is there evil in my family? I cannot help bearing the burden of it. We must come to a similar sense of solidarity with respect to all the larger groups to which we belong. Is the government of my city corrupt? I must carry the burden of this corruption on my own soul. Is there wrong doing and misery anywhere within my reach? I must say to my own soul, ''That, too, art thou!'' The guilt is mine as long as I have talents, time, gold, which I might devote to the bettering of conditions. Thus it is with all our human relations.  We have just one thing to do in life, and that is to build up the kingdom of God.  There is no other measure of success, no other measure of responsibility, no other measure of sin.

# THE CHRIST OF PERSONAL
## EXPERIENCE

# CHAPTER XIII

## THE CHRIST OF PERSONAL
## EXPERIENCE

The issue between the dogmatic and the non-dogmatic views of religion is nowhere else as decisive as it is with respect to the place of the Christ in the Christian life. If, reasons the dogmatic preacher, Jesus not only possesses the moral qualities of divinity, but is himself very God, how can there be any real reconciliation between a man and his Maker except as God is recognized as God in the form in which he has chosen to reveal himself? If the doctrine of Jesus' deity is true, is not a denial of the doctrine a denial of God? Is not even hesitation toward the doctrine identical with disobedience to God? In short, the formula of belief is represented to bear such a relation to reality that acceptance or rejection of it has transcendent practical importance. The inference is, that the doctrinal question must be settled by each individual for himself prior to every other step in the Christian life.

Saving virtue is thus attached to a formula, and one's eternal destiny is made to hang upon the thread of one's orthodoxy. Not only so, but the formula is so constructed as to forbid any genuine investigation of its truth. It allows of no postponement of the conclusion, for any consideration whatever, but commands instant acquiescence. Such is the steely stiffness of the dogmatic view. It knows of no way to follow Christ except the orthodox formula lead the way.

## Must the Doctrinal Problem be Solved in Advance of the Practical?

Fully applied, this theory commits intellectual highway robbery. For it halts us with the command, "Your assent, or your life!" Of course, few preachers have the hardihood to be perfectly true to the dogmatic point of view. They are too close to the heart of Jesus to apply in actual practice such a legalistic scheme, however it may go with their logical consistency. Practically, in fact, the dogmatic scheme is dead. The teachers of the age are telling us that the normal order is not, first know, then do, but just the reverse. Yet the memory of the dogmatic formula abides both within the churches and without. Within is timidity toward the consequences of the newer view; without is a feeling that the Christian religion, as officially represented, is intellectually unfair.

We have already seen what is the nature of discipleship as determined by Jesus' words and deeds. The crucial question with him was never what one holds to be true, even concerning himself, but always what one accepts as one's ideal and makes one's basal motive. "Not every one that saith unto me, 'Lord, Lord,'" but "inasmuch as ye have done it unto one of the least of these." As if to clinch the teaching so as to make plain to all generations the true relation of doctrine to life, he declared that he who wills to do God's will shall know whatever is essential concerning Jesus' divine prerogative.

We have also seen how closely the scientific spirit, which is the antithesis of dogmatic authority, relates itself to the religious spirit. There is scarcely room for debating the question whether there can be such a thing as a duty to believe any doctrine. Such an obligation would be a psychological monstrosity. We cannot say, "Come hither!" or "Go

yonder!'' to the intellect. Or, if we have
any such capacity, it is a power by which man
is able to disorganize his intellect. Whoever
believes a proposition because it is for his
supposed interest to do so commits plain immorality; whoever forms a habit of so doing,
destroys at once his moral character and his
capacity to discriminate the real from the imaginary. This every one will admit, yet many
do not clearly see that the same principle applies to all substitution of emotional need for
strict evidence. Emotional need is properly
an incentive to action, but not to intellectual
assent.

At this point there is to-day especial need
of steady discrimination. It has become evident to the whole world that Christianity rests
upon a far wider basis than that which scho-
lasticism recognized. Emotional and moral
needs are seen to be no less fundamental than
rational considerations. But it is Christianity
as a religion, not Christianity as a set of doctrines, that may properly allow itself to be
determined by the mere sense of need.
Instinctive cravings constitute, of course, an
item of evidence, but this item must be co-
ordinated with all others obtainable before it

is allowed to influence our assent. We must judge of what is true by taking into consideration all available evidence. Other than evidential grounds for the intellectual decision there are none. We must beware, therefore, of confusing the two uses of our instinctive impulses and emotional needs. Their primary function is to induce action. Reflection upon them, which employs them as items of evidence concerning the structure of man and the plans of his Creator, is entirely secondary. Employed thus, they lose their impelling power, and are mere facts to be observed. They are, in a word, inducements to action, but only a part of the evidence for belief.

Nowhere is a consciousness of this distinction more needed than with respect to our attitude toward the Christ. Under cover of uncertainties connected with the abandonment of the dogmatic view, men are evading the practical issues that Jesus has raised. Because the mode of intellectual approach toward the person of Christ is changing, men assume that the practical approach may be postponed to await the theoretical outcome. To undertake to apportion the fault for this mistake would be, perhaps, gratuitous; but it cannot be too strongly impressed upon religious teachers that a slight error in emphasis in their teaching may lead some soul to this disastrous postponement. The Christian church should make clear to the whole world that it has abandoned the dogmatic method of hanging the imperative practical issues of life upon purely theoretical considerations, and that it does not offer to the intellect any substitute for evidence. It must insist that the Christ is so related to us that no intellectual interest or consideration can justly postpone a personal decision in favor of what are, in germ, the essentials of the Christian life.

The Christ of experience, in other words, must take precedence of the Christ of dogma. The concrete, present fact, realized in our own persons, and certified precisely as other personal relationships, must become to us a strictly primary datum, and no longer an appendage of historical or metaphysical insight. Truth is doubtless a single sphere, so that, if we could perfectly grasp the historical and metaphysical truth, we might securely proceed to the experiential applications. But just as surely could we come at the whole by beginning instead of ending with the facts of immediate experience.

In the attempt that is to follow to illustrate this point of view, no effort will be made to define ideal or mature Christian living, but only to show that there is a broad path of genuine discipleship for persons who are still enmeshed in questionings concerning the central fact of Christianity, Christ himself.

## What is the Worst that Doubt can Do?

In the spirit of complete intellectual liberty, let us calmly face the question, What if the worst possible, from the doctrinal point of view, should happen? What if we should become fully convinced that the church fathers, the theologians of all ages, and the unnumbered multitude of Christian disciples who have followed the central tradition have been mistaken in their theory about the Christ? Suppose that Jesus was nothing more than a Hebrew prophet of the highest type, who mistakenly applied to himself the Messianic hopes of his people, and was crucified therefor. Suppose that the stories of his miracles and of his resurrection are mere accretions which the uncritical love and enthusiasm of his followers have added to the true history of his life. Complete the case by believing that his character and his teachings have not the moral perfection attributed to them by their defenders. Grant that these ideal qualities have been reflected backward upon the name of Jesus from the gradually developing moral consciousness of the Christian world. In a word, suppose that for us the historical Christ were to pass away, leaving only the ideal Christ to cling to.

The ideal Christ! The moral implications of this term show how impossible it is to escape what goes under the name of Christ, whether it be God incarnate in flesh, or just a dream of our higher nature. However that name has come to have power over men, we are under obligation to seek to reproduce in ourselves whatever of ideal good it expresses. Ideals are to be not only admired but also obeyed. Now, it is a fact of first importance that the Christ-figure has become the moral ideal of the whole western world. Conceivably the world is mistaken. If, upon consideration, you find that Confucius, or Buddha, or your own father presents a worthier view of what it is to live, then it is your duty to

*The ideal without the historical Christ would soon fade.*

follow this leader rather than the one confessed by the majority. Nothing but the good has any right to command your conduct. If even the Supreme Being of the universe should turn out to be a knave it would be your right to assume, and if need be assert, your moral superiority to him. Any flash of insight into the good, however dim and incomplete, at once lays obligation upon us.

Whoever finds the Christ-ideal a supreme one, has firm standing-ground on the positive side, whatever be his state of mind with respect to all else. Granting nothing but the fact of his own approval of the Christ, whether the Christ be merely ideal or also historical, he faces the immediate duty of becoming a worker for the Christian ideal. He becomes in aspiration and in service a fellow of all true disciples. His fundamental attitude is no longer negative or indifferent, but positive. The Christ has given him something to live for. Without surrendering an iota of his mental integrity, he finds himself, in spite of his doubts, drawn upward and outward by the something, whatever it is, that goes under the sacred name.

Will not the church some day realize her

natural affinity for all souls who thus aspire toward the Christian ideal? We need not ask whether their names are written in heaven in order to know that they are our natural allies upon earth. Their faces are set in the same direction as ours. It is of less importance to inquire what they still lack than to seek how the mustard seed of Christian discipleship already planted in them may be watered, fed, and nurtured until it comes to the blossom.

## The Ultimate Test.

In the upbuilding of such a soul, or indeed of any soul, two further principles of first importance find application. One concerns the ultimate evidence by which the Divine Being is recognized; the other the service which correct belief renders to religion.

A first step in discipleship is taken, as we have seen, whenever, convinced of the soundness of the moral ideal expressed in the Christ, one accepts the Christ-ideal as one's own. This movement away from mere negations and mere questionings is based upon experience as distinguished from doctrine. When the doubter looks within his own conscience, and then gazes at the figure of the Nazarene, he knows that these two bear an essential relation to each other. However it comes to be so, he finds a conception of his true self prescribed to him and embodied for him. He finds himself required to obey. Thus, through an effect wrought within his moral nature, he apprehends the Christ of experience, and he begins to come under the influence of the grace of God.

His growth from this point on will depend upon further applications of the same principle of an experienced correspondence between the demands of his nature and the influence of the Christ. This is the ultimate test of the divine. It is possible to hold that human faculties have no capacity for recognizing God's presence, but with this agnostic theory we are not now concerned. Our concern is to know how, the existence of God being granted, we may judge whether he is really speaking to us through a given historical or ideal personage. We can assert at least this, that the ultimate certification must always consist in some sort of mutual responsiveness between the external fact and something already within us. There is no logically conceivable means by which a conviction of

God's existence or of his presence could be imported into us from without. Convictions are not merchandise to be passed from hand to hand. They are not manufactured, they grow. They are a part of the soul's very life, and they must express what the soul is at the same time that they express more than that. So-called external evidence is, and must be, valueless until it is transmuted into internal evidence, something within us acknowledging affinity for something without.

Thus, the conception of a reasonable religion implies the existence within each of us of something that may be called divine. Gold is tried by gold, and silver by silver; spiritual things are spiritually discerned, and God is recognized by virtue of something within us that is already intermingled with divinity. This something may be unnamed, or even unrecognized; it may be as dormant as any other unused capability; even when it functions we may be as unconscious of it as we are of the circulation of the blood. The consciousness of it may require training. Yet to every one of us there comes, now and then, a voice from beyond the self that sets this chord in vibration. We may misunderstand the voice; we may resist and hush it; but without waiting for our leave, What We Are gives its testimony to the I Am.

It matters little to our present discussion how this fundamental relation of every soul to God be formulated. An earlier type of Christian thought, having declared that human nature is totally depraved, could not help seeing that a completely perverse nature would be totally unable to respond to any approaches of God. Accordingly, a special gift over and above our constitutional capacities was said to be infused into us, or into the elect, so as to make them able to apprehend and receive God. For various reasons later thought has turned away from this theory of a mechanical, occasionalistic, and arbitrary influx of the divine, and has reasserted that God is not far from any one of us, seeing that in him we live and move and have our being.

This thought has become crystallized in the idea of the divine immanence. The doctrine of immanence is little more than a consistent exposition of the ancient belief that God is not only the Creator of the universe, but also the omnipresent Upholder of all things. With respect to man this means that the life which we call ours is never merely ours. In some sense, and to some degree, the divine life functions in ours. We are truly individual, to be sure, and so we cannot be pantheistically identified with God. "Our wills are ours, we know not how." Yet, whither shall we go from God's Spirit, and whither shall we flee from his presence? If we ascend up into heaven he is there, because he is within us; if we make our bed in Sheol, behold, he is there also, because we have taken him thither in our own persons. The glory of living and the awfulness of sin rest alike upon this inseparable union of the divine and the human within every individual.

How all this can be it is not our present mission to inquire, for our concern is with the practical applications of truth. Let us assume, then, that somehow the bottom fact of our being is God, and that, through this inevitable relation to him, there is within each of us an ultimate standard. This is a just and almost inevitable interpretation of indubitable facts of universal experience. Not only in the day of adversity, when the visible things and persons upon whom we have set our heart pass out of our sight; not only in moments of danger or in the presence of death; not only under the spell of sacred poetry or of sacred oratory; not only when the critical judgment yields to social contagion; but whenever we are most ourselves we can, if we are observant, detect something within us that reaches out beyond all that is visible, beyond all that is temporal, beyond all that is mutable or imperfect, and against all apparent contradictions, instinctively asserts that our real self is not this merely separate, particular mode of existence, but rather a life somehow realizing itself in and through the eternal and the absolute. We may call this overplus of our selfhood the Over-Soul, or the voice of God, or simply our higher nature; however we name it, it is the fact that makes religion possible, and it contains the practical test of everything that claims to be divine.

Christianity proposes to satisfy the demands of this higher nature, and upon its ability so to do, and upon this alone, depends its ultimate influence in the world. What we are to think of Jesus is bound up in his ability, or lack of ability, to bring this higher self to a satisfactory self-realization. Experience of his influence in our lives, in other words, gives us an ultimate premise for all our reasonings about him. This premise is not an application of an inference drawn from grounds foreign to itself, and nothing within it depends upon any foreign permission. It exists in its own right, precisely as anything else that we recognize as good.

This is why Christianity is so much stronger and steadier than creeds and ecclesiastical institutions. Not seldom the Christ takes hold of men, not through their thinking and planning, but in spite of all that, and so we are often surprised at the amount of unofficial Christianity in the world. For the same reason—because the Christ is a fact of experience—even when the historical or metaphysical figure fades away, leaving only the ideal, men have still to reckon with a power of the first magnitude. The Christ of experience still abides. Under the name of The Anointed One, something still calls to our dormant spiritual capacities to awake. It makes us incorrigibly dissatisfied with evil in spite of our love for it. It prescribes for life a goal that is self-evident and imperative, and it seems to offer just what the soul desires of courage to work steadily for the highest when postponements and apparent failures are soliciting us to accept as our good something less than the best. In spite of doubts, the Christ-figure calls aloud to the deeps of our nature.

The logical procedure is the same for the doubter as for the believer, namely, to observe whether this, which comes to us under the name of the Christ, works out in practice what it seems to promise. How shall we make such observation? By putting into practice all the ideal good that we seem to discover there. Let us cease the dilettante habit of admiring without acting! If the Christ-figure is half as good as we know it to be, it imposes upon us the obligation of surrendering our life of easy-going respectability for one of strenuous devotion to the ideals of the kingdom of God. The divine without us is to be increasingly recognized by the developing divine within us, and the divine within us is to be brought to our consciousness by exercise. The divine without us is to be *recognized*. It could not demonstrate itself with a club. It will not force itself into our convictions as a cannon-ball breaks through the steel plates of a ship. The whole process is a vital one, and it is mutual, God working in us and we in God. However near God might be to us, we could realize his presence only through the active functioning of our own higher nature.

We ought to refuse to discuss Christology with persons who are unwilling to obey the Christ. When Nicodemus came seeking a discussion of Jesus' relation to God, he was promptly greeted with a demand for obedience to the life that is from above. When John the Baptist sent to ask whether Jesus is the Messiah, the reply merely pointed out the self-evidently good works that were being wrought. Just so, the questioning mind of our time should have its attention turned to the immediate duty that results from such contact with Christ as already exists.

This principle penetrates the joints and the marrow of the avowed disciple not less than of the questioner. There is no religious apprehending of God in Christ except through the active functioning and development of the divine gift within us. Not the affirming of Christ but the experience of Christ is what constitutes the basis of our discipleship. We have a claim to the fellowship of believers only as we share his purposes, his toils, his sufferings with and for the world, finding therein at once our self and our God. An old German couplet has it,

> "Das Kreutz zu Golgotha kann dich nicht
> von dem Bösen,
> Wenn es nicht auch in dir wird aufgerichtet,
> erlösen."

"Only as the cross is set up within thee as well as upon Golgotha can it redeem thee from the evil one."

For most of us, perhaps, orthodox affirmations are far easier than Christliness of life, and so there comes to us a subtle temptation to trust that out of what is easy the hard will somehow evolve itself, that belief in the divinity of Christ will cause the Christ to be formed within us as our life. Without doubt this has been the order of events in many a soul, but it does not describe a causal sequence. The attractiveness and the commanding authority of Jesus depend upon no syllogism, are a product of no proposition. They are not a product at all; they are an ultimate fact. The authority of Jesus is nothing more than the fact that he so infuses himself into every soul before whom he has been lifted up as to make it impossible to be one's self without making him the Master of one's life. He proves his right to us by making it impossible for us to escape him without ceasing to be ourselves.

"For me to live is Christ." To disciple and unbeliever alike comes this all-compelling formula. If we can be our complete selves without him, no conceivable chain of logical reasoning can ever bind his authority upon us. But if, in order to be ourselves, we must follow him, then is his authority as absolute as the ultimate premise of any reasoning process. The Christ of personal experience then becomes the self-evidencing power of God and wisdom of God.

## The Service that Correct Belief can Render to Religion.

The importance of correct belief regarding the historical and the metaphysical Christ is as great as, but not greater than, the contribution that such belief makes to the completing and unification of life. The demand for life is an ultimate one, and conscious life, particularly the life that knows right and wrong and love and hate, presses on to a conscious unification of itself with itself, with its fellows, and with all reality. It seeks to become an integer, a unified whole.

> " 'Tis life, whereof our nerves are scant,
> \*   \*   \*   \*   \*   \*
> More life, and fuller, that I want."

Religion is to be tested by life in its totality, while beliefs are adequately judged by their logical grounds. We require of a belief that it satisfy one side of our being, but religion must integrate the whole of it. The religious significance of a correct belief, therefore, lies not merely in its correctness, and not even chiefly here, but more in its contribution to the unification of life. Similarly, any false belief is obnoxious to religion because it defeats the ends of intellect, but it is also judged by the still more severe standard that takes account of its tendency to disorganize life. If orthodoxy means simply correctness of belief, it sinks into an entirely subordinate place when compared with the whole sphere of which religion is the center and the circumference. He is most religious who most nearly approximates complete living; he is most a Christian whose life, all in all, most nearly reproduces the spirit of the Master.

For doubter and believer alike, there is a relation to the Christ more profound than any that can be formulated in the purely intellectual terms of true and false. It is the relation of a concrete life to the concrete conditions of living. This is not to deny the importance of seeking to know in what sense it is true that Jesus and the Father are one. This cannot be a matter of indifference to religion, for we are made for truth, and wrong belief at this point must certainly tend to maladjustment to the conditions of life. But the degree of our adjustment to those conditions scarcely begins to be measured by the grounds that can be exhibited for our beliefs. Conversely, no proposition regarding Jesus' relation to the Father can express what humanity has found in the Son of Man. Rather, the demonstrated ability of Jesus to organize life is what gives him his supreme rank among men. He brings order, equilibrium, harmony into the personal lives of men, and into the dealings of man with man. He does not repress or deaden our functions, but brings them into action, and develops them to their highest potency. He does not bind us, he sets us free. Were he allowed to control the social, industrial, and civil life of the world, he would bring to its highest fruitage all that is good in civilization. And he does not stop here. He bestows new vigor upon those other aspirations that reach into the invisible and the eternal. In his presence, spiritual things become real to us. In him, in short, is life in its wholeness, and that life, rather than the fragment of it which we call belief, is the light of men.

Thus is the Christ of experience more compelling than the Christ of syllogism. The one is fact, the other is theory. One we are acquainted with as a present, living power in our lives, the other we merely know about as a historical or metaphysical being. This we can say and glory in without casting any slur upon the honest efforts that men make to appropriate the Christ through the logical intellect. We simply refuse to limit ourselves to their preferred mode of procedure. Inasmuch as the modern world has chosen to make its appeal to experience, we meet it on its own ground, saying that experience proves the right of the Christ to the service of our lives.

The traditional plan seeks to develop experience out of the syllogism; the modern scheme begins with experience and makes it the chief basis of its theories. One seeks first to prove what the Christ can do in order to secure for him a chance to do it; the other lets him do what he can, and then asks what kind of being it is that works such effects. According to one, all practical values depend upon the correctness of somebody's logic; the other boasts of treasures so secure that no theory can endanger them.

Let it be noted that these two are opposed in method only. In substance of doctrine they may well coincide. In fact, the appeal to experience has led not a few men to conclude that the Christ of experience can be nothing less than God manifest in the flesh. What keeps our interest in the historical and metaphysical question alive is, indeed, the greatness of the experienced power of Christianity. We go backward into history and upward into metaphysics because we have something that needs explaining. Many a man whom the speculations of theology have left unconvinced has been held back from negations by considering what we already know by empirical evidence. Through our parents or through the church, let us say, there has come to us something that saves us from ourselves and to ourselves. It sets up an ideal end that commands the approval of our whole higher nature, and somehow power streams from it to enable us to aspire and to work. It is no glittering but empty abstraction. It grips our moral judgment and all our moral powers in a vital encounter. Our best thoughts of life have all been better thought out and better formulated before us. As we give ourselves to this Christ and cling to him in loving appropriation of his spirit, we find ourselves empowered for the battle of life, while in proportion as we forget him and turn away from him, we grow weak and discouraged. He has become the life of our life, and so has taken just such a place in our life as would be appropriate for God himself.

It is just such experiences as this that keep alive the orthodox view of the Christ in this age of empirical methods. The objection may be made, of course, that these experiences have been evoked under and by means of the dogmatic process which puts belief first and life second. Certainly it is true that up to the present day of Christian history, the practical influence of the Christ has been exercised very largely in connection with that assumption. But whether the dogmatic point of view was ever requisite to securing these effects may well be questioned. Orthodoxy can luxuriate in individuals and in communions without producing any corresponding control of the life by the Master of Life, while Christly virtues can thrive in individuals who have no opportunity to follow the syllogistic process, in those who take no interest in doctrinal questions, and in those who deny the truth of orthodoxy.

The best and the most fruit will, of course, be produced, other things being equal, in connection with correct beliefs. For right thinking is one factor in the complete integration of life at which religion aims. Yet it requires no very technical information about the human mind to be able to know that Christly lives have been produced in the past, as they are produced now, far less by belief in the divinity of Christ than by a direct influence from him upon the heart and the conscience. The dynamic of our religion is found in the

Christ of experience. The contagiousness of his personality, rather than the compulsion of logic, is what does the work of regeneration. He does not wait to be explained before he draws men to him; it is enough that he be lifted up. And even when he has been explained, it is not the explanation that moves men, but still, as ever, the fact, of which the explanation is only a shadow. The change that is coming over the religious world, then, does not consist in the fact that, whereas men once derived their religion from the creed, now they reverse the process; for human nature has undergone no such transformation as this would imply; rather, the modern man is coming to do consciously what has always been done, and to apply better logic to it.

## The Testimony of Experience.

The proposal to utilize the testimony of experience with respect to the Christ has not always been understood as it should be, doubtless because it is easier to lose one's way in the inductive direction than in the deductive. Men have actually tried, for instance, to experience the truth of dogma. One experiences the atonement; another discerns the distinct presence of each of the three persons of the Trinity! Others testify to such a wonderful change as only a divine being can work, and as this change occurs in connection with belief on Christ, the divinity within it is reflected back upon him.

The last procedure shows some symptoms of approaching the principle that we have formulated under the phrase, "the Christ of personal experience." But it commonly mistakes the path, as do also certain writers upon the experiential evidence for Christianity. In place of a genuinely inductive analysis of Christian experience, we are offered a set of cases supposed to illustrate a doctrine already accepted, and supposed to be established on other grounds. Some of these writers do little more than describe certain religious experiences in terms of the accepted theology, and all of them pick their cases to fit the exigencies of a general plan of campaign. The result is a neutral compound of misunderstood method and half-observed facts.

The traditional system of doctrine was organized upon the basis of certain philosophical conceptions by rigorous application of a certain method of interpreting Scripture.

One cannot so much as understand the terms in which the doctrine of Christ's person is expounded without first transferring one's self in thought to the times and the attitudes of mind out of which it arose. Now, a doctrine formulated thus, without reference to the facts of experience, may be entirely true, but an attempt to verify it by appealing to experience subjects one to the gravest danger of adopting merely the outward form of inductive science, while supposing that one has the method and the spirit of it. Let those pursue this precarious path who prefer it. There is reason for at least toleration, however, toward those who are willing whole-heartedly to risk the entire case for the Christ upon his experienced power to do for individuals and for society what our higher nature calls for.

Let no one object that such persons would substitute mere ethics for religion, or ignore the supernatural element in Christianity, or reduce the Christ to an abstract ethical ideal. As to the supposed reduction of religion to ethics, the case is like that of the law and the Gospel. Jesus came not to destroy the law, but to bring it to its own fulness. Just so, religion cannot be anything foreign to ethics, or ethics anything foreign to religion. Since the sphere of ethics is co-extensive with the concept of the good, ethics cannot complete itself short of prescribing all the laws that tend to the unification of life, while religion cannot conceivably set before itself a higher aim than this. We have here no question of a reduction of one to the other, but only of the genuine completion of both. He who takes Christ as his master will not tarry long in any merely legal view of life, but will go on to realize that the reality of life is in the moving principle of it; and this moving principle, as he will speedily discover, reaches out beyond the visible relations of men to one another, beyond all that is temporal and fragmentary and merely human. He will find that he simply cannot follow Christ without rising above any ethics that can be placed in contrast with religion.

As to ignoring the supernatural element in Christian experience, how often must our religion proclaim that God is love, and that he who dwelleth in love dwelleth in God! The supernatural is discerned by no observation of omens, but by the appreciative recognition of qualities worthy of God. To ignore God's self-manifestation in our moral and spiritual nature, and in whatsoever tends to make it grow, while we insist upon finding him especially present elsewhere, is to dishonor our Creator and the ever-present Spirit. Finally, would it not be a curious conception of God which should forbid him to speak to us as directly as he has ever spoken to saint or to prophet? Did the formulation of the creed prescribe metes and bounds to him? Must he wait for the creed to precede him, or may he come without bell into any heart that honestly aspires toward the things that God loves? To risk the case for Christ upon experience is not to ignore the supernatural, but rather to throw the doors wide open to its influences.

To the charge that this view reduces the Christ to an abstract ideal the answer is, that the whole proposal is to get nearer to the concrete and farther away from the abstract. Bring the Christ to the test of experience, and the abstractions that have gathered about him will evaporate. Bring him to the test of experience, and he will demonstrate that he is a living power. The Christ of experience is the concrete Christ.

The experiential evidence of God in Christ

is, in fact, the most tremendous thing with which the historical and the philosophical investigation has to deal. If we seek data for a theory of the person of Christ in Scripture and philosophy alone, excluding the effects of Christianity as experienced by ourselves and others all through the Christian history, we leave out the most convincing part. We are dealing with a "has been" which may also possibly still "be." We are dealing with what is farthest removed from us, most liable to speculative misconstructions, and least related to our life. But as soon as we make the experienced effects of Christianity the primary and central datum, the inquiry, though it can no longer move along the smooth track of speculation, gains in human interest. We are now wrestling with facts of which we have immediate knowledge in our own persons, and from them interest streams backward to the historical figure whence their inspiration flows. The concrete power of the Christ-idea to-day argues something definite as to its source and history. Somewhere must be found a cause adequate to explain the effect.

We need not doubt that contemplation of

the Christ of experience will yet rediscover all that is true in the speculative dogma. For the divine must recognize the divine, face answering to face as in a mirror. The supreme fact of religion, God in us, is also the supreme consideration of all religious theory. In ultimate analysis, knowledge of God presupposes his self-evident presence. Nothing less than God could possibly demonstrate God to us. This is why the arguments for his existence have had such a checkered career. This is also the truth underlying the assertion of apologetics that we need a revelation. Trace backward any chain of reasonings about divine things, and you shall find somewhere an assumption of God. Here evidence ceases, but here it is not needed. In philosophy this assumption takes the form of a necessity of reason; but if there is any such necessity of reason, it is because we cannot be our own rational selves without sharing in the life of God. In that case, experience of living is experience of God. In apologetic theology, the same assumption enters at various points. The recipients of the historical revelation are represented as experiencing God in self-evidencing fashion, and we are assumed to be capable of judging whether they were mistaken. We can make this judgment with security if God be in us, otherwise not. The evidence of God is simply himself. The evidence of God in the historic Christ is first of all God in the Christ of experience. And so

## We Need a Revival of Christian Experience.

A great deal has been said latterly to the effect that Christianity is a life rather than a system of doctrine; and this is true, but it should not be understood to mean that the Christian life is merely a set of prescribed acts, or even such acts performed from a Christian motive. The Christian life is the act, and it is the motive to the act, but it is more than all this; it is also experience of God in us, the Eternal in the temporal, the Absolutely Worth While that lifts us above ourselves, and transfigures our particular acts and purposes We must find in Christ not merely a stimulus to action, but also the calm of a divine presence, the peace that passeth all understanding. This we shall not secure by seeking for psychical signs and wonders, nor by any theological reflection, but only by learning to estimate the whole of life, and to live the whole of it with reference to the Christian point of view. We must find that the Christ is the vital principle of everything that makes life worth living. In every duty, in every impulse to the good, in every approving voice of conscience, in everything that tends upward in any department of our nature, we must realize that we are face to face with the kingdom of God. Its life and its law is the Christ. Because he is formed within us, our very consciousness of self must come, as did his, to be habitually interfused with a sense of the divine presence. In some sense and in some appreciable measure we must be able to echo his own words, "I and the Father are one."

Such an experience will bring a great calm to souls tossed by the unrest of the age, at the same time that it furnishes incentive and direction to absorbing religious zeal. It will set things in proportion. Act and motive, creed and conduct, self and society, will fall into place. It will give perspective to the theoretical problems that center about the person of Christ. We shall gaze at them without timidity; we shall put no false emphasis upon tradition, or upon our own reasonings, for we shall occupy the standpoint of Realization. We shall conquer sin, too, and win the world to Christ because the Presence goes with us.

# INDEX

PRINTED BY R. R. DONNELLEY
AND SONS COMPANY, AT THE
LAKESIDE PRESS, CHICAGO, ILL.